NO

SECOND
CHANCE!

DISARMING THE
ARMED ASSAILANT

BRADLEY J. STEINER
6TH DAN

PALADIN PRESS
BOULDER, COLORADO

No Second Chance!
Disarming the Armed Assailant
by Bradley J. Steiner
Copyright © 1986 by Bradley J. Steiner

ISBN 0-87364-341-0
Printed in the United States of America

Published by Paladin Press, a division of
Paladin Enterprises, Inc., P.O. Box 1307,
Boulder, Colorado 80306, USA.
(303) 443-7250

Direct inquiries and/or orders to the above address.

Contents

This book is dedicated to my wife, Lin-Li, and with affection, to those few friends who have always meant a great deal to me: Bob Perna, Mitch Miglis, and James R. Jarrett. I also owe a profound debt of gratitude to my many teachers, living and dead, from whom I received much of value:

Professor Kiyose Nakae
Professor Siu Lee
Professor A. Pereira
Charles Nelson
Lt. Col. Rex Applegate
Capt. William E. Fairbairn
Col. Jeff Cooper
Master Young K. Lee
. . . and the others

1
Disarming and Hand-to-Hand Combat in Police Training

The time devoted to training a professional law-enforcement officer is precious—for both the officer and the community he will serve. It is also expensive for the taxpayer to finance the proper training and education of a professional officer.

Every hour of the police recruit's training time is directed at one thing: producing a capable warrior against crime, a protector of society who possesses the physical and the mental equipment and competence to defeat society's dangerous enemies.

Curriculums vary enormously in academies and police schools throughout the United States. They range from the excellent training program offered at the Federal Bureau of Investigation's facility (at the Marine base in Quantico, Virginia) or the Secret Service training center (in Georgia) to the less sophisticated courses administered at local levels by small-town police and county sheriff's departments throughout the land.

Certain areas of instruction are taught to all aspiring law-enforcement officers. Some of these subjects are: the law, and the officer's obligations and responsibilities in enforcement of the law; arrest procedures; police administrative and organizational policy; community relations; firearms training; fingerprinting and identification; and techniques of self-defense.

Disarming, or the physical act of combating a dangerous, armed criminal when one is *un*armed, is taught in various department academies as "self-defense," "jujitsu" (as the FBI calls it), "defensive tactics," etc. Disarming is the most important aspect of weaponless combat training for the law-enforcement officer. Tradition in police training maintains that "arresting holds" or "police come-along" grips are the crux of proper hand-to-hand courses for law officers, but there are several reasons to break with this tradition.

First, come-along holds are effective only when the officer has a decided strength advantage over his suspect and when the suspect is demoralized and will not make a serious attempt to escape. Many years of research with every type of individual have convinced me that the only time an arresting hold will work is when any good hold on the suspect's arm and a growl of "Come along!" would work. This applies even when two officers apply simultaneous controlling grips on a suspect. If the suspect is significantly stronger than the stronger of the two officers, and if he's mentally "psyched" and determined to get free, the hold will not work.

Second, it is not crucial that police officers be able to apply a come-along hold to be personally secure in their work and effective in making an arrest. Taking aim with a sidearm will bring the most belligerent, threatening troublemaker under immediate control as effectively as any come-along grip would, and it requires much less personal risk and danger to the public than wrestling with a suspect. If the criminal does not desist at once when confronted with the officer's sidearm, it is reasonable to assume that he would hardly be unduly upset if the officer attempted a police judo grip.

Wrestling hand-to-hand with a suspect in order to "harmlessly subdue" him is risky beyond any sane man's imagination. This is generally how police get shot with their own guns. (Sociopathic offenders tend to react differently than the way fellow officers do in academy training to the fancy grips that work so well theoretically.)

Disarming, however, is the single most important phase of unarmed self-defense training for the officer.

Disarming trains the police officer to deal with the most dangerous situation a person can face: that of being confronted unarmed by a criminal who is armed, and who would not hesitate to kill the officer.

Disarming training, by its very nature, builds enormous self-confidence when correctly and realistically taught. Officers who develop the ability to confront successfully a knife-wielding lunatic will not be intimidated by a fist-fighter with a big mouth.

Disarming training instills fast reflexes, alertness, a good eye, and keen judgment of timing and distance—all valuable assets in any hand-to-hand encounter, under any conditions.

The purpose of any basic academy course is to give recruits whatever skills they need to keep alive until their own instincts mature sufficiently to enable them to survive under the most adverse conditions on the street.

A realistic, properly administered course in disarming can be an important aid to the officer's own maturation. By confronting trainees with the extreme of what they can expect to encounter on the job, disarming training can bring an appreciation that law-enforcement street confrontations can be fatal.

COMBATO

Here is a brief glimpse of the essence of the Combato (*Jen Do Tao* in Chinese, or the "path of combat") approach:

- All kicks are delivered low, with speed, accuracy, and crushing power.
- Hand attacks stress the speed and fluidity of boxing

and combine this with the lethal power of karate.
- Throws are taught in *combat* fashion only. There is no sporting, judo-type of throw.
- Strategy and tactical approach are wholly offensive, thus assuring speed and efficiency in application.
- Theatrical and fancy methods of applying "restraint" holds to vicious assailants are *not* stressed. Years of research and practical experience have convinced me that such methods do not work.
- The best of combat judo, combat jujitsu, kenpo-jujitsu, karate, boxing, wrestling, the Nelson system, the O'Neil system, and virtually all military close-combat arts are blended into one functional combat method.

Beyond the purely physical skills of the Jen Do Tao system presented in this book, the art places enormous emphasis upon extensive and practical mental conditioning for close combat. This aspect of unarmed combat has just about vanished from most modern martial arts, but in Combato it is stressed to a very high degree.

The system of disarming described in this book owes much to the close-combat masters of World War II: Lt. Col. Rex Applegate, U.S. Army, and Capt. William Ewart Fairbairn, British Military Intelligence, Special Operations Executive (SOE), and famed instructor to the British Commandos, Shanghai Municipal Police and, with Lt. Col. Applegate, master instructor to our wartime Office of Strategic Services (OSS).

One aspect of the traditional martial arts retained in the Combato system is the well-known and widely used belt-ranking system first popularized in Japanese judo and in the Korean, Okinawan, and Japanese karate styles. (The method is also employed in hapkido, aikido, kempo, certain styles of jujitsu, and even in kendo.)

Combato's standards for rank are not comparable to standards in classical judo or karate. A first-degree black belt in Combato bears little relationship to a first degree black belt in, say, Shotokan karate. Requirements are different in the different styles.

First promotion in Combato (to yellow belt) would require a knowledge of how to fall, kick, strike, punch, and block, certain combat throws, and the mastery of twelve multipurpose self-defense combinations. Also, substantial mental preparedness and psychological conditioning of the student for violent confrontations would need to be evident, and steadily improving physical development would be required. For certain pupils (especially women or weaker-than-average men) some breaking may be required, too. The standards are generally high.

The officer need not worry about grades, belts, or ranks. These have value mainly for the instructor to help classify varying levels of student progression. What should concern the officer is learning and practical ability.

The Combato system has little to offer tournament competitors or sportsmen, and it may even irritate some classicists, but there can be no question about the system's value to those who must face deadly danger.

Roughly speaking, three or four classes per week are the desirable number for Combato trainees. Naturally, as with any art, the skills of Combato disarming technique are learned better the more frequently they are practiced. Daily practice is ideal. Three times a week is the minimum.

An officer's mastery of the material in this book will provide the cheapest life insurance obtainable; and it will be the officer himself, even more than his family, who enjoys the greatest dividends from his policy.

Disarming is the one aspect of police combat training that requires consistent philosophy and technique whenever and wherever it is taught. The ruthlessness of the Combato skills in this book should never be modified or watered down, either to pander to public opinion about police brutality or to ease the minds of the more squeamish recruits in the class. Training standards should be kept high, realistic, and aimed at keeping the police officer on the job long enough to retire in good health.

It may be logical to speak of restraint and a more understanding, tolerant approach to nonviolent criminals, con men, shoplifters, *et al.* However, to think that restraint is in order when facing a killer is to make a mockery not merely of police work but of our entire philosophy of jurisprudence.

2
The Law-Enforcement Officer and Disarming Training

In the United States, Canada, and most European countries, law-enforcement officers carry firearms. Officers in the United States generally are equipped with the finest heavy-duty semiautomatic pistols and revolvers and with shotguns, submachine guns, and assault and sniper rifles. In the Federal Bureau of Investigation, the U.S. Secret Service, and some of the larger state-police and highway-patrol departments, training in the combat use of the issue weapons is the finest training of its kind.

The question may arise: why should a member of a modern law-enforcement organization, who is trained to use properly and is fully equipped with modern weaponry, require training in so "primitive" an art as barehanded fighting and disarming?

First, no matter what powerful and sophisticated weaponry is available, there are always situations where an officer cannot make use of a weapon even if wearing one. Only a very foolish person, for example, would attempt to reach for a pistol in a hip holster when an armed criminal was pointing a loaded gun at his head.

Second, every police officer needs to learn to confront with a high degree of self-assurance potentially dangerous, and often psychopathically driven, persons. To do this consistently, and with minimum

7

"wear" to his own psyche, the officer must be a self-confident, tough individual. Proper training in efficient ways to overcome and neutralize stronger and armed men is a simple and superb means toward attaining the goal of solid self-confidence in the officer.

Third, this training reaffirms the need for the officer's self-reliance as opposed to a too-great reliance upon weapons. Weapons of any sort are an artificial, if effective, means of combating the violent criminal, and no law officer should be totally dependent on them. If this occurs, the officer will require a weapon at all times, like a crutch, to keep confidence high enough to perform the job with full efficiency. Every man and every woman who chooses a career in law enforcement must be combat-ready at all times, whether armed or not.

Enhancing fitness, strength, and body hardness is another reason for serious hand-to-hand and disarming training. No matter how sophisticated police and enforcement work becomes, the fit and ready officer will always be the ultimate weapon of the law-enforcement organization.

Alertness, a sixth sense for danger, is a clear advantage for anyone engaged in police and investigative work. This mental attitude is one by-product of sound instruction in disarming and close-combat skills.

The largest law-enforcement organization is never any more effective than its weakest operative. Weakness can be mental, emotional, and psychological, as well as physical.

In the field, whether walking a beat as a uniformed patrolman, guarding the president's life as a Secret Service agent, or raiding the headquarters of a gang of bank robbers as an FBI agent, the professional enforcement officer must have every possible advantage and tool of modern technology and rigorous training at his immediate disposal in order to carry out his mission against crime. Effective unarmed combat and disarming is one of those tools.

There is almost a guarantee that the professional law-enforcement officer will at sometime encounter an armed and dangerous antagonist who must be apprehended or subdued. The officer must know what to do, and must be able to do it fast! The officer in any modern department must know what to do when the choice becomes, by virtue of a violent offender's actions, "his life or mine." An untrained or poorly trained officer is likely to use too much violence too soon, or to provoke a violent incident by projecting inner uncertainty and self-doubt.

A properly trained, fit, and confident officer will tend, by bearing and presence, to discourage rash violence by volatile suspects. (This is not to say, naturally, that mere presence and bearing will always suffice to discourage actual physical assault. However, they will most likely reduce the incidence of such assaults on the officer.) It behooves every conscientious academy instructor to stress these points to all recruits.

An officer who has been well trained in close combat will possess sufficient self-confidence to restrain from physical retaliatory response until and unless it becomes a real necessity. Proper combat instruction will help to restrain an officer who ordinarily engages in violent combat at the drop of a hat: it is the person who feels he needs to prove his adequacy and ability who feels provoked and challenged at the slightest friction.

Many officers, having had their share of amateur encounters (high-school fist fights, general rough-housing, contact sports), look skeptically on martial arts training because of the acrobatic, flashy, and theatrical moves of kung fu, karate, aikido, and so on. Any officer feeling that such showy combat cannot be effective in a real fight will realize that the material of which Combato consists is anything but impractical. The method of hand-to-hand combat in this text is an all-defense method, and there's nothing in the program that isn't workable and effective.

POLICEWOMEN

A physically fit, well-trained woman officer, with the right mental attitude, can learn to fight efficiently with her hands and feet against a male attacker. However, a woman is generally, despite her training, at a disadvantage when fighting a determined male adversary. Aside from the fact that most women are physiologically weaker and smaller than most men, they are less conditioned emotionally and mentally to physical contact and violence.

The greatest advantage any woman has in fighting a man is the element of surprise. With that she can bypass the man's strength and size advantage long enough to neutralize him, if she moves quickly and if she knows what she's doing when she moves. Every ounce of her strength must be brought to bear at the critical instant, if her hand-to-hand skills are to be effective. She cannot afford to hesitate.

The policewoman has special problems in fighting a male attacker. If the methods in this manual are studied with this in mind, and assuming that a conscientious instructor will stress the female officer's need to capitalize upon surprise, speed, and ruthlessness, the policewoman should have little trouble acquiring a working knowledge of disarming skills.

3
Mental Conditioning, Ch'an and Applied Psychology

Most people like living. Staying alive is, for most of us, a self-evidently positive value; we all, even the bravest of us, shrink from circumstances that present the possibility of fatal injury. The person who has chosen law enforcement or similar work is no exception to this fact.

In addition, most people in our culture seem to have a culturally inculcated inclination to make a good account of themselves; as a result of this egotism, most of us demand success of ourselves in any significant undertaking.

We might be tempted to say: "Great! By fearing death (and thus wanting to live) and by needing to prove oneself (and thus wanting to be successful) a student in the West who studies disarming has a natural dual advantage." In fact, the opposite is true. A personal (culturally inculcated or not) philosophy that mixes a demand to acquit oneself under pressure with a dreaded apprehension of death is the worst possible psychological base upon which to build fighting skills for survival.

Under real pressure, the inherent conflict in such a philosophy causes it to break down. If we insist, absolutely assert that we must live, the idea of staying alive will always be the dominant one in a crisis, and we will not withstand extreme circumstances that bring us face to face with the possibility that we may lose our lives.

If we insist that we perform well, then we actually block free-flowing, swift, natural, and effective performance. We prevent good performance because we become obsessed with performance per se, and we cannot function spontaneously. We think too much about what we are doing, instead of just doing it.

The officer who realizes that the very nature of his work places him in almost constant danger has an enormous advantage over the officer who merely sees police work as something glamorous and exciting. However, there must be, along with the recognition of danger, acceptance of the danger, at gut level, or the recognition will lead only to fear—and quite possibly panic—in a crisis situation.

These two concepts that Western man tends to believe and follow are anathema to success in the grim business of serious personal combat and weapon disarming:

- The concept that death is the enemy and that, above all else, one must stay alive; and
- The concept that one must perform well and that when one takes an action (like the action required to disarm a psychopathic criminal) it had better be done correctly.

Often students of martial arts express fear that when "it really happens," they will either forget everything they have learned or be so frozen by fear, they will be unable to do anything they have been trained to do.

In Combato this problem is solved by mental and psychological retraining. Students are taught to rethink their entire philosophy of life, becoming people who will not forget in a crisis what they have learned, or freeze and fail to use what they know. The key to unlocking the student's capability lies in proper mental conditioning, a basic, fundamental premise of Combato.

Police officers are not warriors in the sense that soldiers are, but they are warriors in the very real sense that their purpose is to wage war against crime and criminals. As warriors, it behooves police officers to acquire a workable philosophy—one that will enable them to face the challenges of their work and to survive its dangers.

WORKING ON YOURSELF

Challenge the idea that death is an enemy to be avoided at all costs. Think about death by considering whether it is to be feared or if, instead, it is merely an inevitability to be accepted with calm, inner awareness and peaceful resignation. No one can actually "save" life. When a police officer faces a man armed with a loaded gun and succeeds in overcoming that gunman and siezing the criminal's lethal weapon, there is a tendency to say "the officer saved his own life." Looking at it from the broadest, cosmic perspective, he did not.

Our mortality confronts us from the day we are born, and though we may avoid thinking about it, we never escape the fact. We will die. Perhaps in an hour, possibly not for seventy years, but we will die. Every day brings us closer to our own inevitable demise, and to fear that demise is, in a very real sense, to fear one's own nature as a human being.

Paradoxically, a person who genuinely wishes to be maximally prepared to fight for "life" must completely give up any deep-seated psychological "needs" to stay alive. By being indifferent to whether life or death is the outcome of a fight, as well as furiously determined to fight, one will become a super-efficient fighting machine.

This concept is the root and core of the Japanese art of sword fighting (iaido), a system that, in feudal times, enabled a skilled practitioner to dispose calmly of four or five antagonists with no anxiety whatsoever.

A combat student can conquer fear of death by questioning, challenging, and refuting the basic premises that cause the fear; by meditating on the inevitability of death; and by pondering the irrefutable transience of this life. Acceptance of death can enable us to face even the most dangerous situation with equanimity.

CH'AN

It is imperative to move correctly and swiftly to disarm a potential killer. But the inner demand to "do it right" will all but guarantee that performance will suffer.

Westerners are accustomed to concentrating hard on whatever it is they feel they should do. Simple introspection and recollection will prove that too much "wanting" to do it right can make one apprehensive, and thus ensure that one does it wrong.

Ch'an (Zen, in Japanese) teaches that if you want to see something clearly, do not stare at it; simply let your glance rest on it and absorb it. If you want to do something properly, do not convulse yourself in a furious effort of willpower; just act with all your might and remain emotionally disinterested in the results.

In Ch'an, as applied to martial arts and ways, the object is to act with an empty mind. By "empty," Ch'an refers to a mind free of demands, apprehensions, preconceptions, desires, and, above all, thoughts. By stilling the normally active, "grasping" mind, we can make our natural physical-nervous reactions uncannily fast and accurate—providing that we have, at some previous time, thoroughly taught the subconscious what it has to do when the time for action comes.

The officer must learn hand-to-hand and disarming skills until they are as natural, as automatic as scratching the tip of the nose when it itches. The officer must, in any context outside of actual training, simply forget "learning" and just react, turning over to the subconscious mind the responsibility of "deciding" what needs to be done.

Emotional detachment is necessary for success in combat. Emotions should be subordinated to ruthless, determined action. An initial emotion (hate, fear, etc.) may trigger awareness of a need for action, but the action cannot be emotion-directed. In a crisis, action must come naturally from the depths of self. Overlearned techniques and reliance on natural, trained reflexes should determine action, rather than conscious decision.

As officers acquire skill with the Combato techniques of disarming, they should totally empty their minds when practicing with a partner in the gym. In other words, once a knife defense, for instance, is thoroughly learned by conscious mental and physical efforts, all mental grasping should be thrown away just prior to drill in the gymnasium. Then when the officer's partner "attacks," the officer responds intuitively, not by conscious, rational decision.

Ch'an meditation is a helpful adjunct to any martial arts training, but only when the student understands the purpose of the meditation. Without this understanding, meditation may go on for years, without ever discovering any connection between the two activities. For the modern Western student and for the police officer, the Combato approach of immediately striving for the "empty" (in Japanese, *mu-shin*) state of mind is, in my experience, best.

Combato is not a pure Oriental art. It is a blend of what is functional in both Asian and Western combat systems. Psychologically, Ch'an mental training is an important element of training for combat efficiency, and it is a product of Oriental thought and culture.

Readers desiring greater insight into meditation, or wishing to understand more about Oriental meditative arts in general, may refer to these excellent books:

1. *Zen and Japanese Culture,* by D. T. Suzuki
2. *Ch'an and Zen Teachings,* by Lu K'uan Yu (Charles Luk)
3. *Secrets of Chinese Meditation,* by Lu K'uan Yu (Charles Luk)
4. *A First Reader in Zen,* by Trevor Leggett
5. *How to Meditate,* by Alan Watts

PRACTICAL PSYCHOLOGY

In efforts toward self-mastery and development as a capable fighter, the police officer can use methods to increase psychological abilities that have been in use for decades by practical psychologists.

Visualization and mental imagery can be used to excellent effect by any self-defense and combat student. Teaching a pupil to do this is an important part of Combato training.

We all tend to function in a manner that is congruent with our image of ourselves. If we believe sincerely that we are a certain way, we will act that way. By repeated and continual daily efforts to visualize and imagine physical strength, speed, and flexibility, any person can more closely approximate the ideal, both mentally and physically.

For the police officer, this training can be life-saving. Through repeated and continual efforts to imagine the self without fear, officers can come to accept the conviction that, indeed, they are without fear. They will, with no conscious effort to do so, begin to behave in the necessary manner when placed under stress.

Specialized military units, like the Navy's SEAL Commandos and the Army's Special Forces, are often taught to use a form of self-hypnosis whereby they can convince themselves that they "are" inanimate objects (rocks, a still pond, etc.) so that they can remain hidden and undetected by enemy patrols. In combat, these same elite troops can convince themselves that they are tigers or other ferocious animals—animals whose traits of speed, reflex, strength, and courage are needed to carry out a mission and survive in battle.

Combato incorporates mental training along the same lines used by these elite forces. When learned well and applied in training, results can seem fantastic.

Optimism, positive outlook, and, above all, positive self-imagery must be used by the officer in the mental-training program. Officers must see themselves, and come to feel themselves, as the best. By implementing such steps at self-development, they can actually become what they seek to become.

The best way to implement an effective program of self-training the mind is to make daily efforts of short duration to build one's positive visualization. This may be done at any time convenient to the student.

Police-academy instructors may wish to precede all classes in close combat and disarming with a brief period of this auto-suggestive imagery training. At first, pupils may find it difficult to appreciate how this mental work can affect their physical performance, but as the weeks of training progress, doubts will be resolved.

The secret of building genuine self-confidence is to give people the opportunity to tap their resources and demonstrate to themselves that their mastery in a given area is increasing. This is done by increasingly giving them more to do, and by making progressively heavier demands upon them. Then (congruent with their physical participation), their powerful mental imagery and their positive, dynamic self-suggestions of ever-increasing ability will augment their skills and build a solidly confident fighter.

4
Disarming Techniques in the Combato System

There are radical differences between techniques for sport and techniques for actual combat. Combato has no sporting aspects or aims; as a purely combat-oriented art, it assigns an important place to disarming in the curriculum. Combato pays far more attention to instruction in modern disarming than do karate or the various kung-fu systems, for instance.

Man-to-man combat is war in microcosm. Disarming an armed assailant when the officer has no weapon is perhaps the most dangerous form of man-to-man encounter. A disarming situation is, in fact, a fight for life. There is no second chance. The officer must be alert to that fact.

Combato's disarming procedures derive from methods extant during the 1930s and 1940s when the British and American war effort made training available to special Ranger and Commando units destined for dangerous missions behind enemy lines. The OSS, the Army Rangers, the American First Special Service Force, and the British Commandos all evolved, out of wartime necessity, improvements in traditional martial arts for use in modern warfare against an armed attacker.

It is generally not appreciated just how much

Western experts have contributed to the evolution of the unarmed and hand-to-hand martial arts systems: little-known experts, such as Charles Nelson, for example, who fought on Guadalcanal and who, as a Marine and later as a civilian, worked out marvelously effective manuevers of practical combat jujitsu. I consider Nelson's practical, "Americanized" approach a real boon to the self-defense field. Men like Rex Applegate, William Fairbairn, Eric Sykes, John Styers, Pat "Dermott" O'Neil, John Martone, Wesley Brown, "Izzy" Cantor, Bill Underwood, and the famous Major Kilgore (of the Canadian Commandos) are some of the Western experts of martial arts who easily rate the respect generally reserved for the Oriental masters. I hope that Combato will be the all-encompassing way of Westernized self-defense that wins a place for Americans among the recognized contributors to the spectrum of martial arts systems.

Combato was developed as an all-encompassing Western-Eastern system of effective, practical combat-survival methods; in Combato we use all that is effective from both Eastern and Western martial traditions. The objective of Combato is to modernize, synthesize, and "practicalize" the physical, mental, and spiritual aspects of all forms of close combat.

Fundamentally, Combato consists of three overlapping spheres:

1. mental and psychological conditioning;
2. physical conditioning; and
3. techniques of close combat.

In the combat-oriented martial arts system, each of these three major spheres must receive adequate attention in the training curriculum. The officer must be instructed not merely in the techniques of disarming, but also in the critical psychology of this skill. A suitable self-training program in physical conditioning is important because a high level of physical fitness will aid the officer's development as a fighter.

MENTAL TRAINING

Mental training includes Ch'an meditational practices adopted from the East, psycho-cybernetic and self-image psychology, self-hypnosis, positive thinking, and the "Rational-Emotive Psychology" techniques of Dr. Albert Ellis. The studies of psychopathology, as an aid to understanding the violent criminal, and thanatology, the study of death, are also important.

Mentally educating oneself for personal combat, survival, pain tolerance, and the conversion of fear into anger and anger into action is crucial for the proper development of the pupil's combat-ready state as a totally efficient fighter.

Mental training includes such things as the "combat color code," developing the survival mind-set, programming the psyche for violent confrontations, and tactics and basic combat strategy.

PHYSICAL TRAINING

Physical training includes the development of strength, flexibility, coordination, endurance, and toughness of the body both internally and externally. While the police officer need not participate in physical training to the extent that a candidate for the first degree black belt in Combato does, it is necessary for the officer to get and stay in reasonably good shape.

Combato's physical training includes rope skipping, running, weight training, calisthenics, isometrics, natural-weapons hardening, and more. The end result of adherence to such a schedule is fast reflexes, a high threshold of pain, strength, coordination, explosive power, body hardness, will power, and endurance.

For the combat-oriented martial arts student, great explosive power is the chief physical-training goal; endurance, which is a primary aim of the competitor, is not emphasized.

The importance of physical fitness should be obvious to the student of disarming, and these suggestions are made for the reader's benefit:

1. Follow a regular program of exercise, on a daily basis. One hour per day of regular participation in a vigorous calisthenics course will keep the officer in good shape. Exercises such as chinning, push-ups, sit-ups, rope climbing, in-place running, yoga stretches, rope jumping, punching the heavy bag, swimming, and especially sensible weight-training are all excellent roads to fitness.
2. Maintain healthy bodyweight. Your weight should be what your bone structure can carry efficiently and well. Never "bulk up" by packing on mere fat weight; put on only effective muscular weight—that's all that will help you in a fight!
3. Follow a healthful, balanced diet.
4. Select one sport that you like purely for its own sake, and participate in it throughout the year.
5. Keep a positive, optimistic outlook at all times, and regard any lasting depression, hostility or anxiety as you would a physical injury—something that requires immediate professional help to alleviate. Your mind can keep you fit, or wreck you.

The *techniques* of Combato cover all of the various hand-to-hand combat situations that occur. Combato's moves are highly adaptable, and one basic technique well-learned can be used in as many as a dozen variations.

1. *Basics* are the fundamental kicks, strikes, blocks, punches, parries, evasions and combination moves that are essential to almost all the self-defense combinations in the system. Throws, falling methods and takedowns are also classified as basics.
2. *Attacks* are unique to Combato. They are highly practical and effective combinations of basics, plus other moves and strategies, including tripping, butting, feinting, employing takedowns and holds. These attacks are designed to enable the Combato pupil to take the initiative in an emergency and quickly neutralize any opponent.

3. *Situational self-defense combinations* are actual self-defense combinations that cover all possible forms of assault. When the pupil learns the basics and the attacks, he is prepared for offense; the situational self-defense combinations prepare him to employ defense. These moves are unique because they are *tactically* offensive. There are eleven categories of situational self-defense combinations:

  1. Defenses against punches and kicks;
  2. Defenses against bearhug-type encumbering bodyholds;
  3. Defenses against full nelson, hammerlock, and come-along grips;
  4. Defenses against choking, strangling, mugging, and headlock-type holds;
  5. Defenses from a sitting or lying position;
  6. Defenses against multiple attackers or "gangs";
  7. Defenses against wrist-grab type attacks;
  8. Defenses against rushing, charging, and tackling;
  9. Defenses against lapel, collar, clothing, and hair seizures;
  10. Defenses aginst weapons;
  11. Defense follow-ups when opponent is thrown or knocked down.

4. *Special auxiliary techniques* are highly specialized skills of a military or paramilitary nature. They include use of the knife in combat, the garrote, stick, hatchet, improvised/unconventional weaponry, etc.

While this book presents some very good techniques, they must not be taken by the reader as a sure approach to disarming. Anyone who faces a weapon-bearing assailant is up against a grave danger. Risk is a part of combat, and martial arts teachers who say their method always works are either fools or liars. The best techniques of disarming, when properly learned, will give the student a good fighting chance, no more.

THEORY OF MOVEMENT

There are two basic principles of technique application and movement in Combato. First, use lethal or crippling techniques only when you are under deadly attack. Second, use the techniques in perpetual, barrage-like fashion until the attacker is neutralized.

Combato theory holds that offensive, not defensive, methods will provide the most effective means of countering any form of dangerous attack: when attacked, *attack!*

PRINCIPLES OF DISARMING

The problem of disarming an armed assailant is twofold: first, we have the primary, immediate danger of the weapon; second, there is the living force directing the weapon, i.e., the attacker.

The only sure way to eliminate danger is to cut off the source of the threat. This means that the attacker must be neutralized. All methods of disarming that fail to see this (or refuse to see it) are based on irrational and untenable theory, and are too dangerous to use. For example, there are "disarming" or "police tricks" in the arts of jujitsu and aikido that involve wresting the weapon (knife, gun, club, etc.) from the attacker. These techniques take no cognizance of the fact that the attacker makes the weapon a threat. The attacker is a serious danger as long as he is physically able and conscious. He will fight desperately to retain control of his weapon, and he will never simply allow the disarming trick to work. The weapon-bearer's free hand, his feet, knees, head, and even his teeth, constitute deadly threats to the officer so long as the weapon-bearer remains uninjured and alert. The weapon-bearer *must* be rendered helpless when his weapon is turned aside.

KNOW THE ENEMY

It is vitally important to remember that the armed

criminal always poses a threat to his victim far in excess of the possible injury that his weapon alone may inflict. Remember that the criminal is a living person, with arms, legs, teeth, a brain, will power and adrenalin pumping through his body, and that he wants to win the fight every bit as much as the officer does.

Desperation is one weapon every violent criminal possesses. The desire and determination to avoid arrest and imprisonment can motivate almost supernormal strength and power. The only way the officer can counter this edge is with speedy neutralization of the criminal's capacity to offer resistance; the criminal must be crippled. An attempt to bring an armed offender under merciful control is an exercise in futility and stupidity.

Much is made of nonlethal law-enforcement weapons and the philosophy of minimum force. I think that no obligation to be merciful can reasonably be placed on the victim of any violent assault—least of all on the unarmed victim of an armed assault. (This applies, incidently, not merely to police officers, but to everyone.)

Violent criminals do not display any particular interest in being merciful, and they don't seem to go out of their way to procure nonlethal weapons. Any ruthless, brutal, dirty trick that the victim of an unprovoked armed attack can muster to save himself or herself is justified by the attacker's disregard of human decency.

No matter what the officer's legal restrictions may be, it is reasonable to advocate ruthless brutality when, unarmed, he faces a potential killer with a lethal weapon. Every officer must understand the need for instant, ruthless action, when action is called for.

5
The Bladed-Weapon Attack

Facing a knife in the hands of a vicious sociopath or violent criminal is perhaps the most blood-chilling experience an enforcement officer can expect to encounter. A gun may be technically more deadly, but the average officer would probably prefer to face a loaded pistol than a crazed slashing and stabbing street fighter—especially when, for whatever reason, the officer is unarmed. Desperation, not technical skill, is what makes the violent criminal such a deadly threat when he attacks with a knife. It is ridiculous to assume that any bladed weapon attack may be defended against with little risk because the attacker employs his weapon in an unskilled or unapproved technique.

The officer must learn that when facing a knife-wielder, hesitation means almost certain death, even in cases where the attacker is a juvenile, is unskilled, or is otherwise seemingly inferior. Instructors must emphasize this.

The criminal who attacks with a knife has an incredible advantage over his victim, even when the victim is properly trained: the criminal has already decided to use his weapon ruthlessly, and has the advantage of making the initial physical move. This means that the knife-bearing assailant has both a psychological and a physical edge in the first moment of the attack. It is imperative that officers, most particularly inexperienced officers, understand this grim reality at the outset of their training in knife-disarming procedures. Officers who do not understand this will labor under false premises during training, and will likely carry these false premises into dangerous assignments, with a probably fatal result. Unless this no-nonsense indoctrination accompanies the officer's actual training in disarming skills, it is unlikely that the officer will be able to retain and use the techniques, no matter how good they are, in the field.

There is a world of difference between disarming a fellow officer who poses as the attacker in the police gym and disarming a murderer under actual combat conditions. The difference lies not so much in any noticeable variance in the attacker's basic movement, but rather in the attacker's desperation. The time for the officer to learn to expect to encounter an assailant's fury is during training, not on the street.

This is not said to exaggerate the difficulty inherent in knife defense, or to discourage the officer. Whether we like it or not, the knife is widely used by criminals. If we recognize the threat, we maximize our chances of surviving such encounters.

The neophyte must learn that lethal danger exists the very second a bladed weapon appears in a suspect's hand. There is no time to ponder or delay. The normal tendency to hesitate, so common to everyone not versed in effective and realistic combat methods, must be overcome at the outset of training.

There is a certain cold-blooded psychology that sets the knife-user apart from the criminal who would use his fists, a handgun, or a club to resist an officer. The use of a sharp blade to tear or stab at an opponent takes something above and beyond (some may say below) what the use of a gun or club requires.

Instructors in the military, for example, have found that though a fighting man may fairly easily accept the notion of beating, strangling, or kicking an enemy to death, there is a subconscious resistance to closing with a man and killing him with a knife. Few soldiers can be relied on to use a knife with full vigor, even with theoretical knowledge of how a knife should be used.

It is a matter of life and death for the enforcement officer to appreciate and grasp the fact that a violent criminal views everything from a different perspective than the relatively healthy, so-called normal person. Attempting to reason with a knife-wielding assailant is suicidal. There can be no common ground for understanding, no basis for compromise. The sociopath is untroubled by mutilating, slashing, or murdering the officer.

Distinctions between types of knife attacks need to be drawn. How the attack is made determines which of the appropriate disarming skills (described in the next chapter) will be brought into play. The psychological/mental principle of knife disarming is appropriate for every type of attack, but the physical technique itself varies with the assailant's approach.

THE SKILLED ATTACKER

The single most effective, practical method for employing the knife in close combat was developed by the late William Ewart Fairbairn of the WWII British Commandos. Fairbairn was attached to the U.S. wartime Office of Strategic Services for the purpose of instructing our clandestine operatives in his hand-to-hand and knife-fighting system. Anthony J. Drexel Biddle (instructor to the U.S. Marine Corps and Department of Justice) and John Styers (U.S. Marine Corps) were also prominent proponents of practical and efficient knife combat skills.

An assailant who employs a method of knife fighting resembling the methods espoused by Fairbairn, Biddle, or Styers can be regarded as skilled, however he picked up his knowledge and ability.

Figure 1.

The trained knife-user can be distinguished from the unskilled knife-fighter by the skilled user's effective grip and stance. The grip that a skilled knife-user employs is illustrated in Figure 1. Note that it is a firm but not convulsively rigid grip. It is such that a thrust, slash, or whiplike cut can be instantaneously delivered without telegraphing the knife-fighter's intention.

The stance of the trained knife-fighter enables him

to execute his moves in nearly perfect balance, without committing himself to an off-balance position when he thrusts or slashes. The Styer knife combat stance illustrated in Figure 1 is derived from the fencing stance. The Fairbairn stance is basically the same except that the knife is held in the hand corresponding to the rear foot. Either stance is viable.

A person who employs the approved knife combat grip/stance is a formidable adversary. Combato's disarming procedure and philosophy stresses the immediate neutralization of the attacker, rather than control of him, as is often stressed in many martial arts systems. Any attempt to control or subdue the knife-wielder would be suicidal; any disarming technique that demanded less than a 100 percent effective approach would be absurd. There is just no way that even a highly skilled officer could safely subdue a skilled knife-fighter and disarm him. It might work in an academy demonstration, but it would not work in a confrontation.

THE UNSKILLED ATTACKER

It is entirely possible that a knife assault by a criminal who is unskilled will be more dangerous than an attack by a so-called skilled knife-fighter. Intensity, viciousness, past experience in actually slashing, maiming, stabbing or killing someone, and determination to avoid arrest all must be considered when we seek to evaluate a knife-attacker's capability. There is a gravely dangerous error in the tendency of many instructors and martial arts experts to dismiss so-called unskilled knife attackers as being of little danger to the trained, unarmed defender.

An unskilled attack will generally take one of three basic forms, each of which theoretically prevents the attacker, once he commits himself to a thrust or slash, from altering his course of action. Let us examine the three basic forms of unskilled knife attack.

Figure 2.

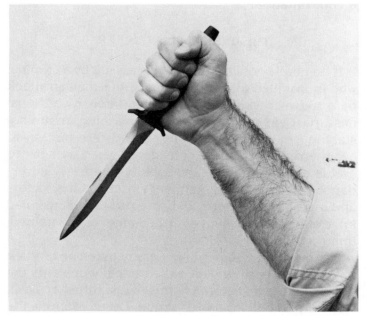

Figure 3.

The Overhead or Descending Stab

It is clear from Figures 2 and 3 that the grip on the knife in the descending stab-type of attack closely resembles the grip normally taken on an ice pick. (Indeed, an ice pick could well be employed in exactly the same manner.)

An attack made with a bladed weapon held as shown is usually directed at the neck or the chest. Such a stabbing attack, if it succeeds, is a tremendous psychological and physical shock to the victim due to the force of the blow. The blade per se is not the only thing to be faced in such an attack; even the short blade of a pen knife carries traumatic shock when delivered with a downward blow, if it connects with full force. It goes without saying that a full-force stab with almost any knife in the neck or chest results in a serious if not fatal wound, but do not forget the danger inherent in the blow itself.

Clearly impossible blocking methods against the descending stab are recommended by many experts (Figure 4). When a defender attempts to stop a descending stab by using his hand as shown, there is a good chance that the attacker's stabbing arm will crash through the defender's grip on the thumb side, and plunge into the target.

The Underhand or Upward Stab

Employing the underhand, or hammer, grip on a knife (Figure 5), an attacker confines the possibility of a vigorous thrust to either an upward stab or a stab directed inward and launched in a wide, archlike swing.

Either stab may be lethally effective if it lands. The force of the stab, aside from the knife itself, is a considerable threat and will produce shock over and above that caused by the blade's penetration.

When the underhand grip is used in an upward stab, the target is the groin or stomach. When the underhand grip is used in a wide, swinging attack, the target is the face, neck, or torso.

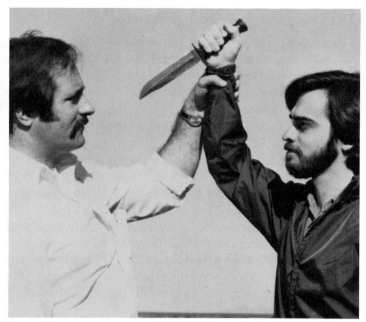

Figure 4.

Figure 5.

The upward stab, like the downward stab, must never be thwarted by a hand-grip type of block. The momentum of a determined stab is great, and it would almost certainly crash through any hand-grip block.

The Backhand Slash

The grip on the knife in this form of attack is basically the same as that used in the descending stab attack (see Figures 2 and 3), but in the slash, the direction of the attack is across the front of the body, rather than downward.

The backhand slash attack, like the downward and upward stabbing attack, generates tremendous force and will deliver great shock to the target if it lands. Target areas for this form of attack are generally the face, neck, or torso.

There is a form of skilled knife manipulation employed by trained combat experts that makes use of a grip similar to the one taken in the backhand slash method of assault. However, the trained fighter will not employ the backhand slash attack. The proper employment of a knife in this fashion is little known outside specialized and highly trained groups of military and police combat specialists.

SUCCESSFUL DEFENSE
AGAINST A KNIFE ATTACK

An unarmed officer is at a critical disadvantage when facing a sudden attack by an opponent armed with a knife. However, providing the unarmed officer has been realistically schooled in effective defense measures, there is a chance for success.

In defending against any knife attack using Combato, no attempt is ever made to stop the knife hand directly and immobilize it. The defender's entire body must coordinate in an action that both maximizes the efficiency of the disarming technique and removes the officer from danger, in case the officer's deflecting move misses and the blade continues in its path.

There may be exceptions to the knife defense under combat conditions, because of the unavoidable un-predictable nature of an attack and the uncertainties generally inherent in self-defense. A life-or-death situation may demand a sort of "trade-off" defense, when, because nothing else is physically possible at the time, the officer must accept a lesser wound in order to avoid a fatal one. (This will be elaborated upon in the next chapter.) The effective basic defense strategy is coordinated body action aimed at immediate avoidance of the weapon's effect and instant and ruthless counter-offensive action against the attacker. Disarming, in the Combato context, does *not* mean controlling the attacker and taking away his weapon. It means averting or avoiding the attack and neutralizing the attacker at once.

A successful knife defense, in a no-holds-barred actual combat situation, hinges upon these key fundamentals:

- Act instantly when faced with the attack.
- Apply a good technique of knife defense with full, unrestrained force and total mental and emotional commitment.
- Follow through and take the initiative immediately in attacking the assailant.
- Be in good physical condition and be mentally cool and sharp.
- Accept the inherent risk entailed in disarming and be fully prepared to get hurt, if it is the necessary price to avoid getting killed.

We may take it as a foregone conclusion that the officer who undertakes to disarm a desperate knife-wielding criminal will get cut. If we expect to get injured we are, to some extent, oblivious to shock when and if the injury does occur. However, if we are determined not to get injured at all, the traumatic effect of any injury is magnified.

So long as the knife-wielder has the opportunity to

continue pressing his attack, he has a strong tactical advantage, with a very powerful psychological advantage, as well. Both advantages must be overcome as soon as possible by the defender, by throwing the criminal on the defensive. This can be done by launching a counterattack at once. With the right physical techniques and the correct psychological attitude, the officer stands an excellent chance of defeating the criminal.

KNIFE HOLD-UPS AND THREATS

When a knife is used to intimidate or detain, the officer's chances for effective defense are superb (see Figures 6 and 7). The criminal who confronts an officer and threatens him with a knife is not likely to know that his victim is a police officer.

When a plainclothes officer confronted by a knife threat has immediate access to the service revolver, it should be used. It is highly unlikely that a uniformed officer with the sidearm in plain sight would be confronted by a knife threat. Most criminals are well aware that the officer need only step back, draw his weapon, and use it. A drug- or liquor-crazed attacker might not realize this at the time, but this would not hinder the officer's correct and appropriate response.

If the officer cannot get the sidearm into action or is not carrying it, and faces a threatening person as shown in Figures 6 and 7, the officer should remember that the man with the knife has not yet made a decision to actually use the weapon. He has therefore placed a block on his own effectiveness with his weapon. He assumes total submission merely because of the presence of the weapon. Futhermore, the defending officer has both the physical advantage (the first aggressive action will be taken by the officer, and not the criminal) and the psychological advantage (which lies in self-knowledge; the criminal cannot possibly guess the officer's intentions).

Figure 6.

Figure 7.

A knife that is held statically in front of the officer can be relatively easily knocked aside, or diverted swiftly, with accuracy and power, unlike the knife that comes under full momentum in a stabbing or slashing action. From the time the blade is diverted, assuming the officer has been properly trained, a crippling follow-up is almost guaranteed successful and would be impossible to either predict or prevent.

The officer or instructor should not conclude that a knife hold-up presents an easy problem for the defender; every weapon attack is dangerous. Still, there is less risk to the defending officer facing a knife hold-up than being the victim of a thrusting or stabbing attack. Psychologically, too, the hold-up man is weaker in his position, for, unlike the criminal who comes in attacking, the hold-up man has not finalized the decision to kill the officer.

There is no alternative for the enforcement officer who is confronted by a knife attack but to counter-attack. Being at all reluctant to do so can only improve the criminal attacker's chances of killing the officer.

TYPES OF BLADED WEAPONS

In the Combato system of close combat (as in the military), the student learns to fight with a knife that is designed specifically for fighting. The most economical is the old WWII standby, designed by William Fairbairn and his associate, Eric Sykes (Figure 8). The Fairbairn-Sykes double-edged combat knife was used by the British Commandos, OSS, American Rangers, and Marine Raiders. During the Vietnam War, it was also official Green Beret issue.

A more modern version of the professional fighting blade is the excellent Gerber Mark II Survival Knife (or its companion, the Mark I Boot Knife). Although not standard issue, the Gerber was popular with many fighting men in Vietnam (Figure 9).

It is true that a fighting knife is preferable for the

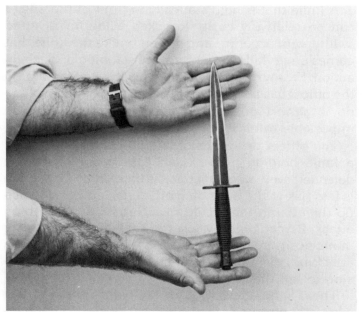

Figure 8. The Fairbairn-Sykes British Commando knife.

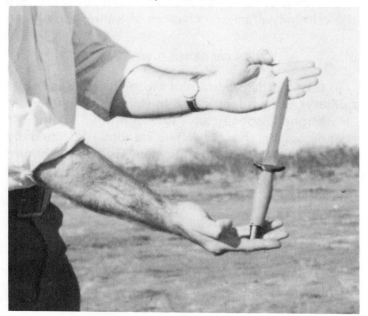

Figure 9. The Gerber Mark II survival knife.

man who carries a knife as personal gear, but the law-enforcement officer should not concern himself with the type of knife his attacker is wielding. He should regard any knife (even an improvised one, like the prisoner's sharpened spoon) as deserving of full respect and instant, violent retaliatory action.

The type of attacker determines the gravity of the predicament for the defender more than the type of knife. An experienced, desperate and hardened criminal armed with a folding knife or a five-dollar hunting knife can be as dangerous as a trained Commando attacking with an approved fighting stilleto.

The styles of knives is an interesting subject from an academic perspective, but no attempt should be made to train an officer to employ certain skills when confronting a fighting knife, and other skills when facing a folding knife. Aside from the fact that such training is utterly unreliable (suppose the officer doesn't have time to tell what kind of knife his attacker is armed with?), it is unnecessary and needlessly complicates matters. The best knife defenses and disarming techniques will work regardless of the type of knife employed. The aim of effective close-combat methods is to make defending oneself as simple as possible.

TARGET AREAS FOR THE KNIFE ATTACK

I believe that the most effective approach in all forms of self-defense is to be *offensive,* rather than defensive, in technique and in spirit. Thus, in Combato, all disarming skills stress an immediate and furious follow-up attack on the weapon-bearing assailant the instant the defender has removed himself from the direct line of the weapon's threat.

Because of this approach, it is best not to stress cover-up when teaching the officers effective skills for disarming. The initial concern is to avert the stab or thrust or slash; thereafter, the concern must immediately become to *counterattack.* While the throat, neck, stomach, heart, inner thigh, kidney, and face are the target areas where bladed-weapon attacks are most likely to be directed, it behooves the officer to structure his repertoire of skills around offensive or counteroffensive methodology. The techniques and methods of disarming represented in Chapter 6 will, when appreciated and mastered, automatically result in maximum protection of the officer's vital spots; they will do so without imposing the tactical disadvantage of being overly defensive. The protection of the officer is of uppermost concern, and this can be achieved only be instilling a spirit and strategy of aggressiveness when the officer's life is in direct danger.

Primed with the right attitude, and motivated to defeat the dangerous criminal, the officer will discover that self-confidence is boosted enormously as skills in techniques of knife disarming and defense are sharpened.

6
Disarming the Knife-Wielding Attacker

The method of dealing with a knife attack described in this chapter is part of the Combato hand-to-hand fighting system. Although the moves derive in part from martial skills extant for many years, Combato offers an updated, practical approach to their physical and spiritual application in modern times.

In Combato it is axiomatic that the defender's last concern should be injury sustained by his attacker, especially when the attacker is armed.

Police officers, being human, are not immune to the same fears and psychological problems of the ordinary person. It is absurd to demand that an officer facing possible death at the hands of an armed maniac conduct himself with that maniac's welfare in the forefront of his mind. There are times in law-enforcement work when an officer is obliged to make a split-second decision to act or perish. When the officer confronts a knife attack, he is facing such a situation.

COMBATO'S BASIC RULES OF WEAPON DISARMING

There are two key maxims necessary to the effectiveness of any given weapon-defense technique:

1. Deflect, block, dodge, parry, or otherwise neutralize

the weapon's immediate threat.
2. Counterattack ferociously and instantly with such fury and speed that the attacker is rendered helpless at once.

Techniques that call for complex acrobatics or for playing with the weapon and the attacker just will not stand up under the frightening, speedy, and unpredictable circumstances of sudden, no-holds-barred combat. Combat does not allow the officer the luxury of "getting set" or readying mind and body for the onslaught. Too often the blade is flashing before the officer knows what has happened.

The officer should never practice any movements that are not simple, practical, and easily executed. What is practiced in the gym tends to become what one will try to do outside the gym, and to try an inappropriate defense in the field could cost the officer's life.

Typical places for carrying a knife are in a sheath carried inside the pants (on one's back) or under a shirt-sleeve, or, when it is a switchblade or folding knife in no sheath at all, in the rear-hip pocket.

Upon stopping any suspicious person, the officer should, of course, maintain a clear view and overall scan of the suspect, especially watching his hands. The officer should verbally command, in a clear, firm voice devoid of threats or sarcasm, that the suspect stand still and keep his hands frozen, in plain sight.

Should a suspect's hand suddenly disappear behind his back or neck, into his pocket, or up a jacket or shirt-sleeve, the officer must instantly launch a whipping front snap-kick into the suspect's testicles (Figure 10). The kick is delivered with the entire instep and with maximum speed and power. The officer must not hold back. Yelling with the kick will increase the kick's power and enhance its shock to the suspect. In any case, following the kick, the officer should follow through by either drawing the service arm or physically continuing with the unarmed attack, in order to gain

Figure 10.

the upper hand and achieve complete control.

The officer *should not just draw the sidearm* when the suspect reaches for an apparent weapon, for two reasons: first, the suspect may be faster in getting his own weapon into play than the police officer would be; second, it takes less time to deliver a hard front-kick than it does to reach for, remove from the holster, level and prepare to fire a weapon.

Downing the suspect quickly may avoid having to shoot him, and it will, more importantly, avoid the tragedy of being shot or stabbed by him.

TWO FUNDAMENTAL KNIFE DISARMING/DEFENSE TACTICS

Chair defense. A chair makes an excellent means of protection against a knife attack. Hold the chair as shown in Figure 11. The chair defense was strongly advocated by Fairbairn and Applegate during the WWII training of the British Commandos and intelligence personnel. Note that no matter how the knife-wielder moves in, the chair provides excellent protection. Don't throw the chair; jab it and move aggressively forward, hard and fast, and thrust it into the opponent.

Throwing an object of furniture is a good move, but it should be done only when, for whatever reason, a more deliberate, accurate attack cannot be made with the item.

Throwing objects and kicking. Anything that can be picked up and thrown is a possible diversionary weapon to use against a knife-attacker. Possibilities include:

- the officer's hat or gloves
- an ashtray
- sunglasses
- a pen
- keys
- a pad
- a handkerchief
- dirt
- sand
- gravel
- a glass of any type of liquid
- a telephone
- salt or pepper
- silverware
- a lamp
- a bottle
- a coffee cup
- a newspaper or magazine

Any item, when flung hard into a man's face, will distract him for a second, and that's all the time needed.

At the moment the object is tossed, you should yell and direct a fast front-kick into the attacker's testicles, or, if you choose, a side kick to break the knee joint is also effective. Immediately following the kick, press the offensive with more kicks, until the opponent is down and out. No attempt should be made to wrestle the knife away from the opponent.

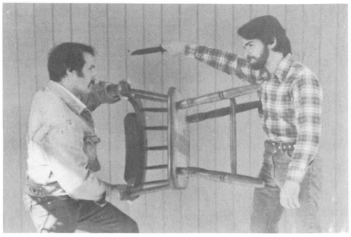

Figure 11.

PARRY-TYPE DEFENSES

To parry or deflect a bladed weapon is much more desirable than to attempt to block the thrust or stab directly. (Blocks are, occasionally, desirable and necessary as defensive procedures, but parrying is the preferred method.)

In Combato, parries are considered maximally efficient when there is some distance between the defender and the assailant. The distance between the two antagonists enables the defender to utilize the necessary body movement and pivotal action necessary to the success of a parry-type defense. Blocking, on the other hand, does not depend on any pivotal movement for success. Blocks are appropriate only as sudden defenses in very cramped and restricted quarters (like a narrow hallway, phone booth, or elevator).

In none of the parrying or blocking techniques described in this chapter should the officer ever attempt to follow up by physically taking away the attacker's weapon. Parrying and blocking should be followed by knocking, maiming, or, under pressing circumstances, killing the attacker.

The effective and well-trained officer will always be aware of and alert to his surroundings at all times. He will strive to keep his back well protected and his hands at the ready, and he will of course never allow himself to be crowded into an awkward or vulnerable position by would-be assailants. Often, in fact, just being aware and alert will suffice to discourage any attempts at physical attack. In any case, the potential killer will be placed at some disadvantage if he tries to assault an alert and ready officer.

To parry effectively, the officer needs to be able clearly to perceive the movement of the blade. If he does see the knife coming, the parry will almost always succeed.

Parrying an attacker's stab or thrust requires a minimum of physical strength, since it involves only partial contact with an attacker's knife arm. The parry (unlike the direct block) redirects the force of the attack in a harmless direction, or one minimally harmful to the defender. While parrying, the body as a unit should move smartly in coordination with the actual deflecting action. Strength for the counterattack is required once the parry has been completed, when the officer's entire focus of concentrated force must be exerted.

Overhand Stab Attack

To parry against an overhand stab attack look at the attacker carefully as he moves in (Figure 12). This is extremely important; the need to keep your eyes on the assailant must be stressed throughout training.

As the knife, in this instance held in the attacker's right hand, descends, step quickly to the right-rear of the assailant with an upward-inward sweep of your own right arm against the attacker's arm (Figure 13). This sweep will redirect the force of the stab in a safe direction no matter how great the force is (Figure 14).

At the instant the parry is applied, your counterattack must commence. Several forms of follow-up may be applied from the completed parry position.

Figure 12.

Figure 13.

Figure 14.

1. Using the thumb-side ridge of the parrying hand, or the forearm, snap your hand up suddenly into the attacker's nose or throat (Figure 15). Follow up with a left hook punch, augmented by a full body twist, into the attacker's kidney area (Figure 16). Then seize the assailant with your left hand from behind (by grabbing the collar, hair, ear, etc.) and direct a hand-edge chop at the right side of the opponent's neck (Figure 17). This shocks the vagus nerve and carotid artery. Deliver a kick to the back (hock) of either knee (Figure 18), as you yank him backward, bringing him briskly to the ground. Once on the ground, the stunned attacker is vulnerable to heel stomps to the head, a kick to the ribs, armpit, neck, etc. And you should proceed without hesitation to use these techniques for final control.

2. By drawing your right knee up to your stomach after the parry, you are in a good position to side kick the attacker's knee. Following the side kick, chop with

Figure 15.

Figure 16.

Figure 17.

Figure 18.

your right hand at the assailant's kidney or at his head. Turning to face the attacker as he falters or topples, reveals the spine, kidney, ribs, or head of the opponent as targets for continued attack. When the attacker is actually down, the knife-wielder should be dealt kicks and stomps.

3. After parrying, step in close behind the opponent and rake and tear at his eyes with your right hand and fingers (Figure 19). As this snaps the attacker's head back, a right-hand chop across the throat will end the encounter (Figure 20). Once downed, use your feet against the assailant, until he is neutralized.

A variation of the parrying movement can be applied against the right-hand downward stab by using the left hand and arm. Here, you dodge off to the right side of the attacker with your left foot, as your left hand sweeps up and inward to meet and divert the stabbing attack (Figure 21). After completing the parry, you are in a position to chop the assailant across the nose with

Figure 19.

Figure 20.

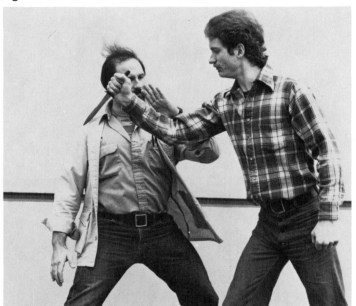

Figure 21.

your left hand (Figure 22). This is followed by a hard right-elbow shot or right-hand punch into the ribs (Figure 23). Following the punch or elbow strike, the opponent is brought down with a kick to the hock of the knee. More stomps and kicks are used when the attacker is actually down.

When the left-hand parry described has resulted in the opponent being propelled forward from the momentum of his own lunge, the best follow-up is a hard kick to his tail bone (coccyx) (Figure 24), followed by further kicks.

As long as you adhere to the basic plan of parry and attack, you may change the sequence of actual moves described. The specific combinations of attacks given here are only recommendations; it is the principle that you should retain, rather than any single, definite move. Do not attempt to take away the attacker's knife!

Obviously, all techniques in this section (and in this entire book, for that matter) must be mastered for both

Figure 22.

Figure 23.

Figure 24.

right and left sides. The wise officer will lay particular emphasis upon training the weak side.

A Straight-In Thrust Attack

As the opponent thrusts with his right hand, pivot quickly on your left foot, swinging your left arm inward and your right foot backward (Figure 25). As the knife thrust is deflected, sharply pivot in close to the attacker and deliver a hard right punch into the ribs or kidney area of the attacker (Figure 26). Follow-up can then proceed in a manner described under the downward-stab defense techniques.

In an alternate parry, dodge to the left as a right-hand thrust is made, and then sweep your own right hand inward to deflect the blade (Figure 27). The resulting position makes a hard semi-roundhouse kick directly into the attacker's testicles very effective (Figure 28). Continue with follow-up techniques.

Figure 25.

Figure 26.

Figure 27.

Figure 28.

An Upward Stab Attack

The upward stab is parried by sweeping the right arm down against the assailant's right arm (Figure 29). A shift of the body to the left should accompany the parry. A kick to the opponent's testicles (Figure 30) combined with hand blows and kicks are the correct follow-up measures.

The upward stab may also be averted by pivoting away and sweeping the left arm inward (Figure 31). From here, a ridge-hand blow across the nose or eyes is effective (Figure 32). Follow with a left hook punch into the kidney.

KNIFE DEFENSES USING THE BLOCK

Blocking a knife attack means meeting the force of the stab directly. It is the least desirable way of dealing with the knife attack. Unfortunately, the block defense must be studied because a sudden stabbing

Figure 29.

Figure 30.

Figure 31.

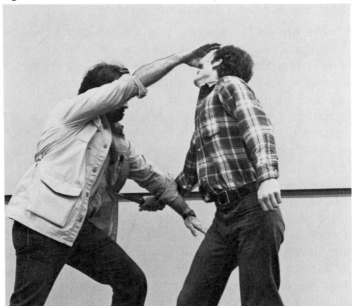

Figure 32.

attack may be launched by surprise, catching the officer off-guard, and the block defense involves minimal movement. If blocks become reflexive, they can easily save the officer's life when other forms of self-defense are impossible.

Knife blocks require courage, aggressiveness, and physical strength; these attributes must be developed in a proper training program.

Blocks should be made by driving one's body weight into the blocking action. Timid, half-hearted efforts to block a determined knife stab will fail. Nothing but an all-out effort will succeed. The officer must realize that there is nothing to lose by throwing everything into defense when facing a sudden knife attack in cramped quarters: injury or death will surely follow otherwise.

In Chapter 5 the wrong way of attempting to block a stab (grabbing the attacking arm one-handed) was discussed. The error of attempting such a defense must be clear.

Forearm Block of Downward Stab

The karate "knife-hand" blow should not be used when blocking a stab; use the forearm, near the wrist. The reason for this is that, while the hand should be open (thus allowing the edge of the hand to connect if possible), it is better not to depend on the small hand-edge area when the larger forearm stands a greater chance of contact. It is easier to throw full body weight and strength into a forearm block than with the hand edge.

To defend against the sudden stabbing attack from above, drive in hard and slam your forearm in and against the attacker's descending wrist (Figure 33). Going staight in makes this a viable defense even in the most cramped quarters. If you can, seize the attacker's arm following the block. Otherwise, just keep your forearm pressing against the attacker's arm as you deliver a vicious knee blow to his testicles. At the same time, drive a powerful jab into his chin with your free

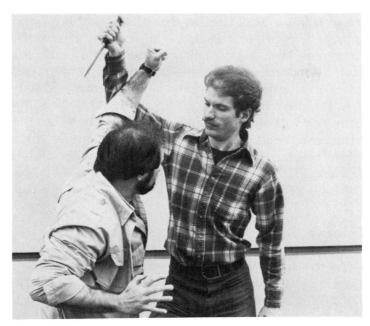

Figure 33.

Figure 34.

hand (Figure 34). The fingers of the jabbing hand attack the eyes after the blow is struck. As the assailant crumples, step back quickly and deliver a hard kick to his head, repeating the kicks until he is harmless.

As an alternate counterattack to the downward stab, you can drive in hard, blocking against the offending arm, and without hesitation drive your elbow into the attacker's head, trying to crush the temple area. Simultaneously, drive a knee blow into his crotch (Figure 35). Step back as the attacker falls and follow through with a barrage of kicks to vulnerable areas.

Forearm Block of Upward Stab

As the stab ascends, drive your left forearm down hard against the attacker's right wrist (assuming a right-hand stab attack). It is imperative that you block directly into the attack (Figure 36). Drawing the forearm back prior to snapping it down will make the block too slow and permit the stab to penetrate to its target.

Instantly, as the block connects, your right hand, fingers extended and stiffened, drives into the attacker's eyes (Figure 37). A front snap-kick to the testicles (Figure 38) should drop the assailant. Step back and follow through.

In an alternate defense, the block is made against the attacker's right-hand stab with your right forearm (Figure 39). Immediately following the block, sweep your blocking hand down and to your right, as either your right instep whips a kick into the crotch or your fist punches into the solar plexus (Figure 40).

Follow-up is made by closing in and either raking the attacker's eyes with the left hand or chopping across the bridge of his nose with the left hand.

At close quarters, when you execute a front-kick, it is sometimes desirable to let the shin, rather than the instep, connect with the opponent's testicles.

Figure 35.

Figure 36.

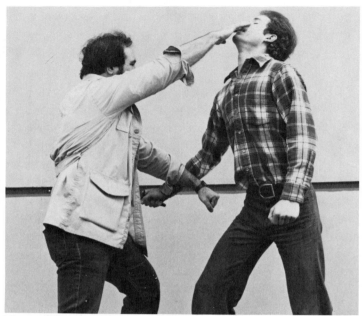

Figure 37.

Figure 38.

Figure 39.

Figure 40.

Forearm Block of Straight-In Thrust

The straight-in thrust is the most dangerous at close quarters since it is most difficult to block. When you detect the beginning of the attacker's thrust, drive your forearm in and down hard against the lower forearm and wrist area of the knife hand. At the instant you lunge forward to block the thrust, your opposite (in this case the right) hand either punches or seizes the assailant's testicles. A head butt could also be used in stunning the attacker for the moment. As an alternative to the testicle blow, thrust your free hand in a finger-spear thrust into the opponent's eyes.

Once the attacker's thrust has been neutralized, press the offending weapon out of the way and continue with attacks to vital spots to render the adversary helpless.

The likelihood of sustaining a stab or cut wound during any knife attack is high; you should be prepared for such an eventuality. A stab in the arm is better than a stab in the throat or in the midsection, and considering that death is the alternative, a cut on the limb is nothing at all.

That a weapon defense may be concluded without sustaining any injury is, of course, possible. However, you should be mentally prepared, any time you face an edged weapon, to receive an injury.

CROSSED-ARM TYPE BLOCKS

In many traditional karate circles, crossed-arm blocks are popular (Figures 41 and 42). However, I think that they are not reliable as primary block defenses, except against club or kick attacks. Since the main advantage of these blocks is power, they are more practical for women officers. These blocks tend to be slightly slower in execution because crossing the arms takes time—time that simply slamming one arm forward does not take. Any adult male sufficiently fit to pass a police department physical exam should have

Figure 41.

Figure 42.

the power to execute one-arm blocks.

Knife stabs usually come at terrific speed. Kicks are rarely if ever delivered as fast, nor are club swings. So it would be here that the crossed-arm blocks should be used.

Any officer who feels a natural predilection for the crossed-arm type blocks and can apply them instinctively and quickly (which only a good instructor can ascertain) should use them against knife attacks.

Follow-up is the same as for the blocks previously described.

KNIFE HOLD-UPS

When a knife is used to threaten or intimidate, it is less dangerous than when it is in motion.

The officer need remember only three rules to deal with a knife hold-up:

1. Knock, kick, push, parry or strike the knife aside while retaining a grip on the knifer's wrist or arm if possible.
2. If the knife hold-up is from behind, glance back to see which hand the knife is in before moving.
3. Follow through furiously with rips, kick, chops, and punches at vital points.

A knife held at the throat, from in front or behind, is a dangerous threat (Figure 43). However, if the officer knows that the opponent will use his weapon, action is imperative. After a fast sweeping block and grab of the knife arm (not to remove the weapon, only to help stabilize your balance), deliver a front snap-kick to the opponent's crotch (Figure 44).

In a critical situation, it is better to grab the blade itself, fully knowing that the hand will sustain a bad injury: by seizing the blade with total concentration, you may gain a second in which to turn it aside and follow up.

Figure 43.

Figure 44.

7
The Bludgeon Attack

Because the nightstick (baton, billy, riot stick, police club) is standard issue for most U.S. police departments, the officer is doubtless familiar with at least some aspects of how a stick or clublike weapon is used in combat.

Generally, a club is not as feared as a knife in close-quarters battle. It is certainly true that a trained man can easily kill an unarmed opponent with a stick, but a stick is usually easier to defend against than a knife.

The officer is usually more willing to close with, and attack, a man with a club than he is a man with a knife, and this is a great psychological advantage.

THE UNSKILLED STICK FIGHTER

An officer is most likely to encounter a club attack where the bludgeon is used in a wild, unskilled manner to strike a forceful downward blow on the head of the defender. Such an attack can be dealt with relatively easily, providing the officer is not taken by complete surprise, and assuming a reasonable level of physical fitness and mastery of proper defense techniques.

THE SKILLED STICK FIGHTER

An enforcement officer is unlikely to encounter an

expert stick fighter. Stick fighting as a martial art requires enormous discipline and dedication, both physical and mental, over a long period of time. Most criminals and violent types are not willing to follow the way-of-life approach to achieve combat skill mastery in the Philippine, Javanese, or Japanese stick arts.

An officer might expect to encounter an ability to use certain tricks of stick manipulation. Anyone who is fit and capable of applying basic stick techniques is certainly a formidable adversary and is to be regarded with respect, but it is not true that he is an expert, nor is he impossible to beat.

The stick, as a weapon for hand-to-hand combat, offers these advantages to its user:

- greater reach than the stick-wielder would have without the stick or club;
- a much harder and more lethally potent striking point than would be available from "natural" weapons, i.e., hands or feet;
- the psychological edge from having a weapon available when one's opponent has none, or when, as in the case of a police officer, the weapon may be holstered and immobile.

The stick offers two forms of attack that may result in immediate and serious injury to the officer. First, the strike may be used as a "blow" against a vulnerable target area. Second, the stick may be used to jab like a rapier and deliver extremely punishing attacks to the eyes, throat, solar plexus, groin, etc.

The stick is a versatile weapon. In the hands of an untrained combatant, once the defender averts the initial thrust or strike, it is merely so much wood (or pipe, etc.). However, in the hands of a skilled stick fighter, the unarmed, inexpert defender, taken by surprise, stands virtually no chance of offering a successful defense. It is like a gunman approaching an officer from a distance of fifteen feet with a loaded pistol and shooting; nothing can be done.

The officer whose mental and physical equipment is sharp, who is properly trained, and who uses the training without hesitation can almost certainly defend himself efficiently against any stick or club attack.

THE STICK STRANGLE

The stick strangle (Figure 45) has no place in police work since it is not the officer's job to kill silently; the job is to protect self and society and to make arrests. Officers, however, should be aware of how a stick may be used against them; always keep your back guarded. There are many methods of using a wire, knife, and so forth from behind a victim that leave even a combat expert totally helpless. Officers must appreciate the vital need to stand where there is back protection.

THE OFFICER'S ADVANTAGE

The criminal who is armed with a club has an advan-

Figure 45.

tage over an unarmed officer, at least initially. The offender has greater reach, potentially greater power in the strikes and jabs he can deliver, and a psychological edge, knowing that he is armed and his victim isn't. But with correct thinking and a vigorous course of action, the officer can turn the attacker's advantages against him.

The club cannot fire a missile, as a gun can, nor can it inflict any injury on its own, as a bladed weapon with its edge can. If the person wielding the club does not direct all his attention and all his physical power to its employment, the threat to the defender is nil.

Therefore, the officer need not feel at a terrible disadvantage when facing a bludgeoning weapon. Once the criminal has committed himself to his attack, the officer need merely explode into a counteroffensive; victory is almost certain.

Once the club or stick is dodged, blocked, checked, averted, or parried, providing follow-up is instantaneous, the stick is harmless and the defender has the advantage. In the next chapter we shall study the best techniques for actual self-defense against the stick or club.

TYPES OF STICK WEAPONS

There are perhaps thirty different police-type riot sticks. They vary in length from about eighteen to thirty-six inches. They vary in strength from the very light, almost balsawood batons used by military police, to rugged hardwood types filled with lead. There are even rare telescoping bludgeoning weapons, such as those used by European resistance fighters during WWII; such a weapon also was used by the U.S. OSS.

Simple dowels, while not being the very best implements for hitting, can easily kill when manipulated in trained hands. Pipes, steel bars, hammers and mallets, or table legs may be used as lethal striking implements.

Like the knife, the club depends to a large extent on the user for its effectiveness. A really vicious killer armed with a broom handle is a greater threat than a harmless loudmouth who picks up a tire iron and brandishes it menacingly. However, an obviously unapproved type of weapon should not cause the officer to relax his vigilance.

Lead-filled saps or "persuaders" are dangerous weapons, but few criminals use them. They are weapons designed for close-in work, almost like brass knuckles, and their advantage is one of increased power, not reach. By becoming adept at the defenses presented in the next chapter, and by learning the basics of general hand-to-hand combat (fist defenses), the officer will be able to cope with a blackjack attack.

With the element of surprise, there really is no defense against a properly used lead-filled sap. The recipient of a full-force blow will be down and out and in no state to offer any resistance. Again, remember the need to be alert; you can meet an attack that you see coming with an excellent chance for successful defense.

METHODS OF DEFENSE

The officer must begin to learn club disarming by learning that all attacks must be regarded as life-threatening, and that all defenses must be so foolproof and easy to master that they can be applied in a wide variety of combat situations and executed quickly, instinctively, and effectively.

Techniques that call for bringing the club attacker under arrest control without actually hurting him are theoretically attractive to many. The problem with such techniques is that there is no way to read the mind of an attacker. We cannot determine if he is cowardly and likely to submit as soon as a hold is clamped on him, or if he is a wild-eyed psycho, intent on maiming or killing his victim. When the man on whom a come-along grip is used jabs his fingers into the officer's eyes, kicks the shins, and breaks free, it is too late to realize that the come-along grip was inadequate.

A weapon in the hand of an offender should trigger the red-light attack signal in the officer's mind and reflexes. No man who employs a weapon criminally and aggressively deserves any consideration whatever. He is a potential killer, and the officer must be conditioned physically and psychologically to regard him as such before it is too late. Disarming techniques employed against a club attack must, like all other types of disarming techniques, be ruthless and decisive.

The club attack is met first by blocking, dodging, or turning aside the blow. It is easier to block a stick than a knife, because once the stick has been averted it is useless to its user.

Obviously, the police officer who is issued a riot stick should be trained in its proper use. Though not strictly disarming technique, I think a brief discussion of proper stick technique will be valuable. Also, familiarity with how a weapon is used correctly helps teach correct defense against that weapon.

The officer should appreciate the stick's capability but not think of it as an invincible weapon. With this attitude, the officer will learn to use the stick realistically.

The stick is a superb weapon against an unarmed perpetrator, and a pretty fair equalizer against a bladed weapon or against another stick.

Figures 46 and 47 show the proper way to utilize the thong in holding a nightstick. The thong is first looped over the thumb; the hand is then turned and the baton grasped. The officer needs to be wary of any of the "control" grips popular in some circles, which use the long riot baton. No violent criminal who means business is going to stand still and allow such a hold to be applied. It is far better, when control is desired, to bring the perpetrator down with a smash across the

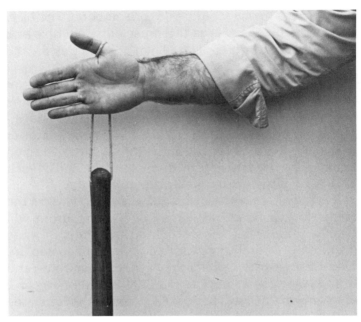

Figure 46.

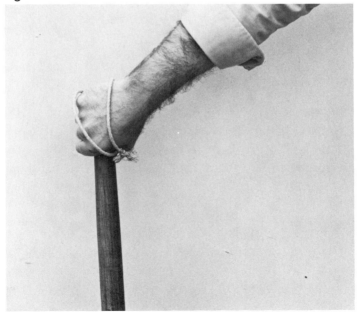

Figure 47.

thigh biceps muscle (Figure 48) or shinbone. The blow across the biceps causes the muscle to convulse and cramp in a painful spasm. Then simply put on the handcuffs.

When facing a potential belligerent, hold the baton across the waist at the ready (Figure 49). One foot is slightly back, giving greater balance and maneuverability. From this ready position it is a simple matter to jab into the solar plexus or the throat; break the shin bone; strike the kneecap, the temple, or the neck; block a kick or a punch; or break the collarbone.

If an adversary moves in and attempts to wrestle the stick away, a head butt or a knee in the groin will usually change his mind. Kicking the shins or knee (Figure 50) or stomping on the opponent's instep are also effective when an opponent grabs your baton and tries to grapple. When the criminal is pulling on you, at least one knee will be locked straight; that one may be broken easily with a kick.

Figure 48.

Figure 49.

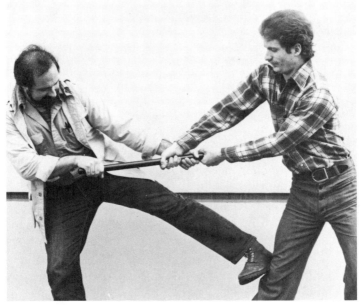

Figure 50.

Even if the officer does not carry or use a baton, it is worthwhile for him to become acquainted with basic baton methods.

8
Disarming the Bludgeon Attacker

Once the bludgeon has been blocked, averted, parried, or dodged, the winner of the fight will be whoever is faster and more ruthless.

If a defender is taken totally by surprise and hit, it may be all over for him. However, unless the club attacker succeeds in approaching his victim from behind, a surprise attack can be almost completely discounted. The officer must regard alertness as the first line of defense. Then he need not worry about a man with a stick catching him by surprise.

THE KEY MOVE

The natural tendency when facing a man armed with a club is to increase the distance between yourself and the stick-wielder. The unconscious reasoning is, "If I can get out of the attacker's reach, he can't hit me with his weapon!" This is wrong. In fact, it is exactly the opposite of what needs to be done.

One advantage of the club as a weapon is that it increases the user's reach. When you back off from a club attack, the attacker maintains the advantage his weapon gave him initially. You must understand the need for going in fast when confronted by a bludgeon—this does not mean you should walk into a crack in the skull, but it does mean that the core of successful strategy here is moving in.

INITIAL STOP-BLOCKS

Instruction in defense against a stick attack should begin with one basic fact concerning the weapon itself: a stick that is immobilized is useless as a weapon, and immobilizing an opponent's stick before it is swung or jabbed is the most positive defense move.

To make effective use of the principle of the stop-block, it is necessary to remember the key move of going in fast. Unless you really commit to a lightning attack when confronted by a club-wielder, the stop-block will be impossible.

Attackers (except skilled stick fighters) usually pause momentarily before thrusting or striking. (This is similar to the unskilled fist-fighter who cocks his fist prior to punching, thereby telegraphing his next movement.)

Begin stick-disarming training by simple drills in stop-blocking. Have one student play the attacker and one student play the defending officer. Ideally, in training, the attacker should be armed with a real nightstick or length of dowel. (I think the popular rubber batons used in martial arts classes are not sufficiently effective training weapons to instill real confidence.) The use of real nightsticks or wooden pieces, however, can be a problem if students are not careful and if they do not follow instructions.

Drill #1:

The attacker faces the defender with stick in hand. Suddenly he raises the stick as though he were about to make a side-downward type of swing (the most common). The attacker does not carry through with an attack; he merely poses for a hypothetical attack.

Instantly, the defender in this drill lurches forward, eyes on the attacker, in a balanced, crouched, forward-

Figure 51.

leaning position, and drives a strong, controlling block into and solidly against the attacker's forearm (Figure 51). No follow-up should be made. This is a set drill only, to condition instant response. Students should take turns as defender and attacker. Twenty attacks per student, per side, is a good drill session. The contact made during the block will serve to harden and condition the arms of both recruits.

Drill #2:

The attacker poses quickly for an inward-type attack. The defender instantly drives in against the attacking arm, stopping it before it gains any offensive momentum.

Again, as Figure 52 shows, the actual block-contact is made arm-to-arm. The defender's eyes remain on the opponent. This is extremely important, and one of the valuable lessons to be learned from this drill. By always keeping his eyes on his attacker, the defender is

Figure 52.

Figure 53.

Figure 54.

instantly primed for the most important part of the defense: the counterattack. No block by itself should ever be relied upon to stop an aggressor in a serious fight. The counterattack is everything!

Twenty repetitions per side, per person are adequate for a training session. Never favor one side over the other in mastering techniques. Learn to be ambidextrous as far as hand-to-hand combat goes. "Combat-ready" means ready on both sides, not merely the strong side.

BLOCK DEFENSE #1

As the attacker launches his downward swinging attack (Figure 53), you respond instantly, moving in fast and slamming a quick, hard block against the assailant's club arm (Figure 54). Your body weight must assist the block with coordinated movement that augments the block. Your head is guarded by the form of block shown. This type of Combato block presents no danger to you if the club strikes down across your back, or even if it glances indirectly off your head. The block is safe as long as your head is guarded by your arm and body from receiving the main force of the blow.

No attempt should be made to take away the attacker's club. Do not try to apply an arresting grip after the block is executed.

One type of follow-up is to drive a powerful knee blow up into the attacker's testicles; as the knee lands, a chin jab follows with all the force you can muster (Figure 55). Follow through by gouging the eyes.

Alternately, after the block, a ripping-type of finger assault may be effectively made against the assailant's throat (Figure 56); or a stiffened finger thrust can be made into the eyes.

It is feasible, while moving in for the block, to kick the attacker's shin bone and/or instep, thus insuring that, even as the block is launched, the counterattack is under way.

BLOCK DEFENSE #2

This technique is a bit more sophisticated as a dis-arming move than the first technique, but it is also simplicity itself in execution. Move in fast at the first sign of the attacker's offensive gesture with the stick. Block hard as your body drives directly at the attacker (Figure 57).

Upon blocking, wrap your blocking arm around the attacker's club arm, thus pinning it helplessly to his side (Figure 58). This provides an enormous advantage for the counterattack: By pinning the attacker close to your own body, you ensure maximum potent delivery of your follow-up measures, and the club is rendered useless as a weapon.

Follow through with a knee to the groin and a chin jab (Figure 59). Since the attacker will be locked into position, you may apply a second knee blow easily and use eye gouges to good effect.

Figure 55.

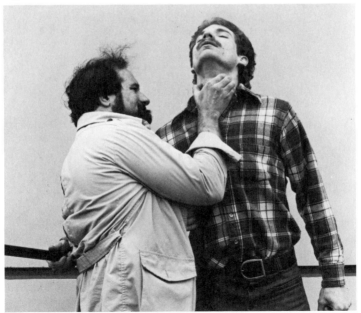

Figure 56.

Figure 57.

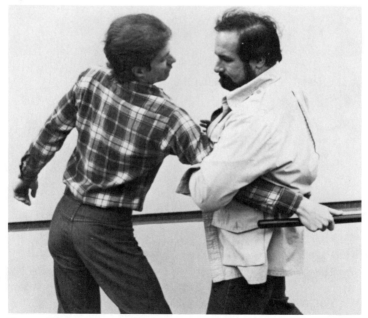

Figure 58.

Figure 59.

PARRY DEFENSE #1

This parry works well against the direct overhead smash. With practice it becomes possible to avoid the attack of the strongest person, using relatively little of your own strength. Parrying is a good defense whenever there is room to move about. When there is distance and the swing is coming in at you, parry! When the opponent is up close, block.

When you parry, you redirect force rather than stop it. Obviously, anyone of slight physique or limited strength would benefit by becoming adept at parrying procedures.

As you see the descent of the club in the attacker's hand, shift to the left (same side as the attacker's arm). As the body shift is made, sweep upward with your left arm, meeting the club arm in its path of descent and following through by swinging the arm down and away (Figure 60).

Figure 60.

It is not necessary to grasp or take hold of the assailant's arm. If possible, fine; if not, the defense will be effective, providing the follow-up is fast and brutal.

Once the club attack has been met with the upward swing of your arm, the counterattack must begin at once. Your position relative to the attacker at the actual moment of parrying will determine the specific follow-up movement. It would be an error to dictate a rigid defense pattern, since no one movement will always be applicable under the varying conditions of combat.

These follow-ups are equally effective, providing that speed, power and determination are behind them:

- At the moment of the parry, kick with the ball of the foot into the adversary's groin or stomach.
- The front-kick may also be applied with the instep to the testicles.
- If the position permits, a side kick can be delivered on the same side as the parrying arm. Kick to the

knee joint, in a hard, thrusting, downward motion that uses the thigh and hip muscles.

- If, after parrying, you find yourself facing the adversary's side, a very good counterblow is a left hook punch into the kidney or ribs (Figure 61); make it strong!
- A somewhat more spectacular counter, but nevertheless practical and effective, is a knee blow snapped into the attacker's stomach or ribs with the knee on the same side as the parrying arm (Figure 62). Grip the assailant's hair, face, clothing, or shoulder with your free hand to assure strong balance.
- An intuitive follow-up is a hand strike with the parrying hand directly up and into the attacker's face. This could be a palm-heel smash to the chin or nose, a finger stab to the eyes, or even a ripping grasp of the opponent's face.

Figure 61.

Figure 62.

These follow-up moves are merely the first of a barrage-like series of counterblows that must be made for certain protection. One of the gravest errors students of self-defense make is the assumption that one or two simple tricks will suffice to overcome an enraged attacker.

At the outset of training the officer should concentrate on mastering the basic parry move itself, plus each of the follow-up steps described. In time, the officer will have a solid foundation of skills to call upon reflexively in a crisis.

Follow-up should be applied according to the "feel" of each given situation. Here are some additional follow-up procedures:

- Following any of the initial countermoves described above, apply a double-hand grasp on the attacker's head and snap him backward sharply, wrenching his neck as you bring a knee up into his kidney or spine area. A chop across the windpipe with the side of the hand can then follow. As the attacker falls, apply kicks and stomps to the head, ribs, groin, or knees.

- A Japanese stranglehold, or the more vicious Combato adaptation of it, is indicated whenever you have stunned an attacker momentarily and moved behind him. Figures 63 and 64 show how to apply the basic Japanese stranglehold. The hand behind the attacker's head jams his head forward while your other arm applies pressure against the throat. The Combato variation is the application of the same basic move, but the technique is applied as a snapping or jerking wrench on the neck, which breaks the neck.

- Following a parry defense and initial counterblow, a takedown executed by tripping the attacker back with the leg, and pulling him down with both hands, is excellent. You should apply kicks and stomps to the downed assailant.

Figure 63.

Figure 64.

PARRY DEFENSE #2

The previously described parry defense employs the arm that corresponds to the same side as the attacker's; the illustrations have shown the defender using the left arm to parry the attacker's right-handed blow.

An effective parry can be applied with the arm diagonal to the attacker's arm. Thus, when you face an attacker who swings with his right hand, you can effectively parry the action with your right arm.

Always keep in mind that a parry depends in large measure for its success on body movement coordinated with the parry itself.

If the attacker has his club in his right hand and moves in swiftly, his club arm descending, step off slightly to the left as your own left arm sweeps, palm open, across the front of the attacker's body.

Your right palm meets the descending club arm as the body smartly pivots away from the path of the blow (Figure 65). This parry will totally deflect the club to

Figure 65.

a position that poses no threat. Then, you must
follow-up.

This parry does not require that the parrying hand
catch hold of the arm of the attacker. If some fluke
allows you to get a grip on the attacker's arm, great,
but it isn't necessary. Instructors should not stress that
the defender grab the attacker's wrist.

Several follow-ups can be applied after this parry:

- the nonparrying arm may deliver a punch or hard
  strike to the attacker's face or throat;
- the parrying hand may rip up and back at the
  attacker's eyes;
- the front-kick can be delivered;
- the side kick can be delivered;
- in addition, you should consider how all the
  previously described counters may be used for this
  second type of parry.

Throwing, tripping, and repeated blows are called
for in an effective follow-up.

Figure 66.

OTHER DEFENSES

Defense Against a Sideways-Inward Swing

To defend against a sideways-inward swing, move in, blocking the club arm either before or just after it starts moving, and follow-up with appropriate kicks and blows (Figure 66).

Defense Against a Backhand Club Attack

Figures 67 and 68 clearly show an effective block and counter to a backhand attack. Use both hands to block the backhand-inward swing, then grab the arm with one hand. Chop your attacker under the nose or across the throat with your other hand.

Figure 67.

Figure 68.

Figure 69.

Ground Defense

The attacker's ankle is hooked by one of your feet and you follow through with a hard kick, using your other leg, to the assailant's trapped knee joint (Figure 69). Every effort must be made to rise quickly from a prone position. Do not grapple on the ground in hand-to-hand combat.

9
The Handgun
Attack

The semiautomatic revolver is the ultimate hand-held, concealable weapon. There is no certain defense against a firearm.

In the United States, law-enforcement officers who receive training from a state or federal law-enforcement agency are well-trained in the two primary areas of police handgunning: using the handgun as a weapon of close combat; and using the handgun as a tool of arrest. But this chapter is not intended to teach handgun use; my concern is how to face a sidearm in a criminal's hand, when the officer is unable to employ armed resistance.

The criminal who uses a handgun to execute or to assist in the execution of a crime may be an hysterical teenage punk or a lethally cool, psychopathic professional murderer. The victim may think it academic to draw distinctions, but it always helps to know one's opponent.

An effective police officer must have highly developed intuition to interpret voices, mannerisms, etc. There is no other way to gain an educated guess as to the intentions of the gunman.

Watch the eyes of the gunman: They will hint at what is on his mind before he acts. The more "mad" (in the clinical sense) a criminal is, the more cold his stare will be. A man who looks at another as he would look at an inanimate object is definitely to be respected as a potentially cold-blooded type. The term "predatory stare" really means something to the trained and perceptive combat professional. The potential murderer has a dead and utterly ruthless tone to his eyes and face.

Does the gunman's voice seem to convey a sense of urgency? If so, does this urgency communicate a desire to get away with the goods or to get the job of killing over with? Determining this requires a good deal of receptivity to the voice and the verbal expressions of the gunman.

The time for wishful thinking is not when one is facing a gun. It is absolutely crucial that you not attempt to allay your own anxiety by falsely deceiving or reassuring yourself when confronted by a gunman. If the facts indicate that escape or money are the only goals of the gunman, fine. If the facts and your intuition say otherwise, then the chance must be taken to disarm the criminal. It is not a situation in which you can abstain from decision making. You do risk death by attempting a disarming move. However, if the facts say that there is a strong chance of being shot, then the risk is worth it.

A professional killer is not necessarily a greater threat than an inexperienced teenager. Professionals kill for money or survival. Amateurs kill out of fear, because they lose self-control, or for psychotic "thrills." An officer confronted by a professional gunman and not shot outright has a definite psychological advantage for disarming. A man with a gun and sufficient advantage to get the drop on an officer could easily have killed the officer; if he does in fact hold the officer at gunpoint instead, the officer can take advantage of the gunman's (possibly temporary) wish not to kill the officer, and he stands a terrific chance of successfully disarming him.

The inexperienced gunman is dangerous because he is not fully in control of himself and is—even to himself—unpredictable. An officer confronted by a clearly nervous gunman should act and speak deliberately to control and allay the fears of the gunman, and to make the gunman believe that the officer is subdued and scared.

Facing the experienced gunman, the officer must be like a professional actor—overdoing fearfulness or being too submissive could be disbelieved by the gunman and cause him to suspect a disarming attempt.

Assume that whoever is holding the gun will use the weapon. Never, never allow yourself to think "he's bluffing" or "he'd never *really* pull that trigger."

These comments about an experienced and an inexperienced gunman are offered for psychological insight. They do not take into account technical skill with the weapon itself. It is true that gun skills exist that make it extremely difficult to disarm a gunman. But nothing is as formidable a barrier to successful handgun disarming as a quick trigger-finger backed by either hysterical fear or ruthless, murderous calculation.

THE SIGNIFICANCE OF TYPES OF HANDGUNS

In Combato, the repertoire of handgun disarming techniques is not based upon firearm type. (This is a departure from certain theories of pistol disarming commonly accepted by police and military instructors. Some disarming skills ask the defender to jam back the slide on an automatic pistol, or to slip his thumb in front of the revolver's hammer if the weapon is cocked. Aside from the fact that such actions are almost impossible to do successfully with real speed, even under well-lit, ideal classroom conditions, they do not offer solidly damaging countermoves.) Forget about disarming techniques that call for special approaches to specific types of weapons. These skills are uncertain, complex, and impractical to employ.

The Combato approach to disarming requires only that the handgun be dealt with, not that the officer stop and determine the type of handgun he is facing. As the techniques of countering a pistol are covered, it will be obvious that the make of the perpetrator's weapon is irrelevant.

TWO STEPS FOR SUCCESSFUL HANDGUN DISARMING

Combato teaches that an effective handgun disarming technique consists of two parts. First, redirect the weapon and/or your body from the line of fire with a vigorous, surprise controlling movement which immobilizes the weapon. Second, instantly following the first step, neutralize the gunman himself, by crippling or killing him.

In Combato, the gunman, and not the gun, receives the defender's full attention once the weapon has been redirected by the initial disarming movement. The officer should never attempt to wrest a firearm away from a conscious assailant. Methods of disarming and self-defense that advocate acrobatic, flashy techniques of taking firearms away from criminals are too dangerous to use for actual combat.

The officer must remember that the skills he is learning will be needed under the worst conditions of stress and terrain, if they are needed at all. Methods of close combat must be workable even under conditions that favor the gunman.

There may be instances where it is desirable to actually disarm a criminal in the literal sense of taking his gun away. We will explore the best way to do this, but wresting away the weapon must always be accompanied by inflicting at least severe pain on the gunman. Otherwise, the officer will invite failure in his disarming attempt, and failure in this context almost certainly means death.

MENTAL CONDITIONING

The person who faces a loaded gun in the hands of

a psychopath faces the possibility of agonizing pain or death. Often the victim of a gunman has time to think about the gravity of his situation too long— longer than in a knife or stick attack, where the situation requires instant action based on learned, conditioned, reflexive skill.

Facing death, the mind is our strongest ally. To face an armed criminal with a 100 percent ready body and a turbulent, unsteady mind clouded by fear is to face that criminal already defeated. Reflexes, no matter how finely tuned physically, are mind-directed. No part of the body moves without a nerve-stimulus to action. No nerve-stimulus to action can be triggered by a fearful, unstable mind.

The student of serious combative disarming must achieve the ability of emptying his mind at will. All preconceptions, all mental grasping must be eliminated for disarming to be effectively undertaken. All human beings possess to some extent a sixth, intuitive sense. This sense enables a person to "feel" that someone is watching, for example; it enables a gunman to "feel" his victim calculating a defense.

The officer's mental conditioning will be at least as important to effective disarming techniques as the skills enumerated in Chapter 10. Facing the gunman with a nongrasping mind (see Chapter 3) is absolutely imperative; nowhere can this method be better learned than from meditational procedures and training. Obviously, this is easier to say than to master and apply, but the job must be done.

Combined with a correct mental state, the pupil must appreciate the importance of relaxing the body as completely as possible. Physical relaxation and a nongrasping state of mind (Ch'an) go hand-in-hand to prepare the defender to use the physical techniques of disarming. Mental and physical readiness is the foundation for disarming firearms. Without it, the most exotic techniques of firearm defense are worthless.

PHYSICAL RELAXATION

Training is needed because proper physical relaxation in the face of an armed criminal bent on murder is not easy. Relaxation makes it possible for the defender to move with optimum speed. It makes it possible for the defender to conceal any hint that a disarming technique will be executed. Since you "telegraph" nothing, the gunman perceives nothing. Relaxation also makes follow-up possible with minimal fatigue. Relaxed, we can fight all day; tensed, we tire rapidly.

Everything said about the correct mental state for disarming and proper physical relaxation must be transposed into the lessons described in Chapter 10.

Practice of handgun disarming should be undertaken with real guns. Obviously, this needs to be done under the supervision of professional, responsible, meticulously careful teachers. Guns may be loaded with powder-filled shells stuffed with cotton wads, for special training. This is not an entirely safe method of training, since the wads are fired in flames and can cause injury. Still, this method of training has much to recommend it. It is as close to actual experience in combat as we can get without using loaded guns.

Goggles must be worn to protect the eyes if cotton wads are employed. When empty guns are used, naturally, no protection is needed.

Blanks should *not* be used in disarming training: at point-blank range they can kill like real bullets.

Remember: All guns must be checked, rechecked, and checked again by both teachers and recruits, prior to their use. The risk entailed in using real guns in training is more than offset by the maximum preparedness and, ultimately, in the lives saved later on.

10
Disarming the Handgun Attacker

The techniques described in this chapter are effective and practical regardless of the type of handgun used by the gunman. These skills will work whether an opponent is armed with a .357 revolver, a .45 automatic pistol, a snubbie .38 Special, or a six-inch barreled hunting revolver.

In studying any form of disarming, but most particularly firearm disarming, the defender's life is on the line. Police officers have to accept that this is a hazardous profession and that in the course of duty it is not merely possible, but highly probable, that they will have to fight for their lives. Death confronts the police officer in the field as it confronts the soldier in battle. The competent police instructor will help his charges accept this fact during the weeks at the academy.

Training in disarming should not be conducted exclusively under ideal conditions. Naturally, the pupil needs to have as little trouble as possible during the basic learning stage of his study; the mechanics of the techniques should be taught, practiced, memorized, and painstakingly rehearsed in comfortable, well-lit workout areas, under "ideal" conditions. The application of the mechanics must never be perfected in this way, however. After the student has acquired a thorough mechanical proficiency in the movements, they should be perfected under much more realistic training conditions.

Practical rehearsal of handgun-disarming techniques should be undertaken outdoors, in dim light, total darkness, cramped hallways, alleys, elevators, offices and other indoor areas. An effective training course in disarming will allow the pupil to gain experience under all possible conditions, even in the rain. The result of such an ambitious program will be saved lives. Every officer thus trained will evidence superior confidence and self-reliance.

Gym clothing should be worn for initial practice lessons: loose trousers (without a belt), a strong, long-sleeve sweatshirt, and sneakers.

Once the pupil has mastered the basics, gym clothing should occasionally be replaced by the clothes the officer will wear on the job, or plainclothes. An officer who is not fast, efficient and strong in regular clothing will not have street-level confidence.

BASIC PRINCIPLES

Disarming should never be undertaken unless there is an intention on the part of the gunman to shoot. Many killings occur because the person facing the gunman attempts to fight to save a few dollars. Use disarming to save lives.

Kidnapping and hostage-taking constitute a clear threat to life. The survival rate of kidnap and hostage victims is not impressive. In any case, the odds are better that a good disarming tactic will work than that a victim will live to talk about his experience.

Relaxation of the body and emptiness of the mind maximize surprise and speed. Control the distance to the gunman as much as possible: an opponent whose gun hand is within reach is easier to disarm. If possible, move slightly during the initial moments of the confrontation, while surrendering, to subtly adjust distance for a possible disarm.

Never glance at the gun before moving!

Never excite, challenge, or threaten a gunman. Agitating a weapon-bearing opponent in any way is courting suicide.

If ordered not to move, don't.

Don't start a disarm at the moment when the order is given to raise your hands (or freeze, or "stick 'em up"). This is when the gunman is expecting resistance.

Acceed promptly and meekly to the gunman's demands. Then, unless ordered to keep your mouth shut, *talk* to the gunman. Speak pleadingly and imply total submission in what you say and in the way you say it. Do not show panic. Panic may alarm the gunman and make him shoot you out of fear that you are going to do something desperate.

Naturally, you will feel some genuine fear, though training will have helped here. In any case remember that your action to disarm will be faster than any reaction on the gunman's part, and that you will choose when to move, and there is no way your antagonist can predict that you have any intention other than submission.

I frankly think that the officer confronting a psychopathic killer should face bluntly the fact that we all will die one day, and that if this is the time "to go" then he will certainly take the killer with him!

FRONTAL GUN DISARMING

In the two-step method of handgun disarming, first remove your body from the pistol's line of fire while retaining control of the gun hand and redirecting the weapon itself, in a vigorous, controlling action. Then neutralize the gunman instantly, and make no effort to wrest the gun from his grip.

Pistol Aimed at Midsection

The gunman may press the gun *into* your stomach, or he may simply point it *at* your stomach (Figure 70).

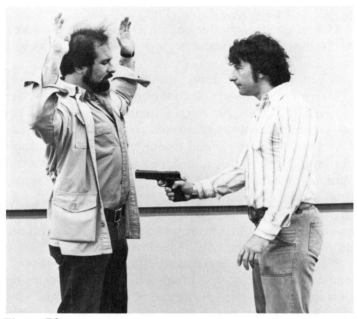

Figure 70.

The disarming technique works well in both instances.

Look the gunman in the eye. Do not twitch, glance at the gun or lower your arms before moving into action. Sweep-chop downward suddenly with your left arm (Figure 71), smashing the inside of the gunman's wrist with the edge of your hand or with the bony part of your forearm, just above the wrist. Drive your knee up into the gunman's testicles (Figure 72) as you deliver a chin jab with your right palm-heel (Figure 73). Encircle the gun arm as shown with your left arm (Figure 74) even if the gunman is not still holding his pistol. With pressure on the opponent's gun arm and a vicious downward blow behind his neck with your right hand (Figure 75), snap his head forward onto your right knee, crushing his face (Figure 76). Deliver an edge-of-the-hand chop across the back of the gunman's neck with your right hand (Figure 77). Deliver another chop across the kidney with your right hand, as the gunman drops.

Figure 71.

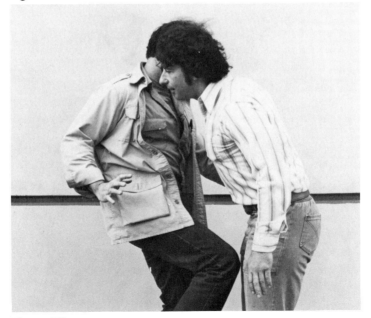

Figure 72.

Figure 73.

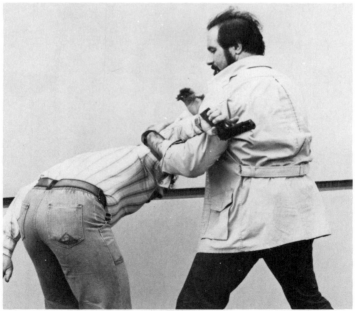

Figure 74.

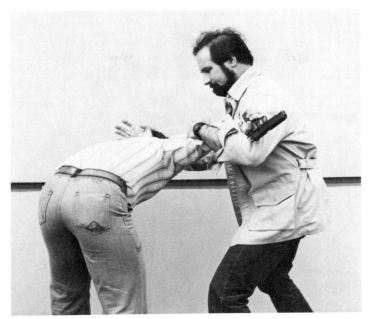

Figure 75.

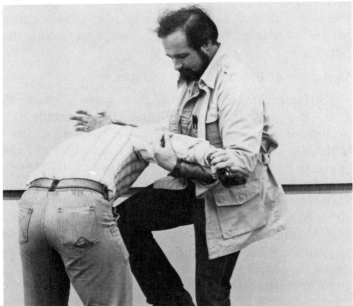

Figure 76.

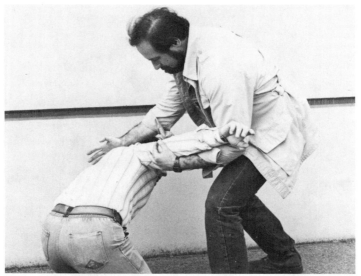

Figure 77.

If the gun has not dropped, and depending upon the position of the attacker, you will now either take away the pistol if he is unconscious, or you will kick him senseless before making any attempt to secure the handgun.

Variation of Frontal Pistol Disarm

You are confronted from a slight distance (Figure 78). Chop the gun hand aside (Figure 79) as you thrust a straight fingertip spear hard into the gunman's throat with your right hand (Figure 80). Grab and hold the gun arm as shown in Figure 81 whether or not he drops the pistol. Deliver a powerful snap-thrust kick with your instep to the gunman's groin; as the kick snaps back, drive your foot into his shinbone or knee. As the gun-man crumples, chop the side of his neck with your right hand. While retaining a grip on his gun hand, break his arm at the elbow with a hard chop or forearm blow from your own right arm. Deliver more kicks and stomps until it is safe to take the pistol away and bring him in.

Figure 78.

Figure 79.

Figure 80.

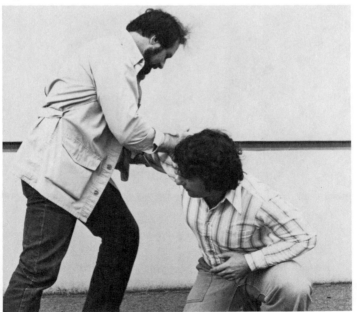

Figure 81.

Disarming from Hands Down Position

Although it is always desirable to respond quickly to a gunman's command of "Hands up!" and although the hands-up position is in fact excellent for both relaxing the gunman's mind and readying for disarming, every officer must be fluid and adaptable to all possible situations. Therefore, being able to disarm a gunman when your hands are down (Figure 82) is important to learn.

Look the gunman easily in the eye. Make no hard stare, and be careful not to give telltale gestures. Do not glance at the gun before going into action.

During this—or any—disarming maneuver a good opportunity for initiating action is when the gunman relaxes and starts to speak. The reason for this is that no one can fully concentrate on more than one thing at a time. All that is needed to gain the advantage in any disarming technique is that quarter-of-a-second,

Figure 82.

initial, surprise move. The gunman who does not shoot his victim outright because he doesn't want to do so has obliged himself to be defensive. He *must* wait for his victim to resist before he fires. Action is always faster than reaction. The disarm *will* succeed.

The first move is a lightning-quick snap inward of the wrist (Figure 83) of the hand on the same side as the gunman's weapon hand. Simultaneously, pivot out of the line of fire and seize and stabilize the gun hand with your other hand.

Maintain an iron grip on the wrist with the right hand. With the left hand chop back hard across the nose bridge, eyes, or throat (Figure 84). As the chop whips back, use the left hand to seize the gun hand to augment your right hand (Figure 85). At the same time, your left foot executes a low, powerful side kick into the knee or shin area of the gunman's right leg (Figure 86).

After the kick immobilizes the gunman's leg,

Figure 83.

Figure 84.

Figure 85.

Figure 86.

preferably by breaking his knee or shinbone, jerk the gun hand up and to your own left, then down, breaking the gunman's wrist and possibly his arm as well. Retaining a strong grip on the gunman's wrist, step back wide and turn to the right, twisting the gun hand over and wrenching the wrist in a painful lock (Figure 87).

Maintaining your grip on the gun hand, deliver a fast front-kick to the gunman's head. Finally, drive a kick with the heel into the downed gunman's face or head while pulling up on the gun hand (Figure 88). Only when the attacker has been rendered harmless should you attempt to take the gun away.

Pistol Aimed at Head—Hands Up

From the hold-up position (Figure 89), pivot away suddenly from the gun's direction of fire while sweeping the pistol hand aside and grabbing it (Figure 90). Viciously kick with the instep into the gunman's crotch, using either foot, and use your other hand to help grip the gun hand (Figure 91). Deliver a second hard kick into the attacker's groin or knee (Figure 92). Execute a chop across the nose, throat, temple, or nape of the neck, whatever area is exposed (Figure 93). Follow up with more incapacitating techniques.

Figure 87.

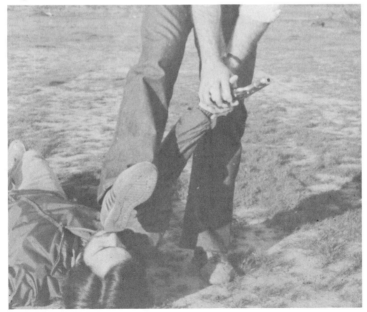

Figure 88.

Figure 89.

Figure 90.

Figure 91.

Figure 92.

Figure 93.

Pistol Aimed at Head—Hands Down

When a pistol is aimed at your head while your hands are down (Figure 94), dodge quickly by stepping to the side and in. Reach up and get a grip on the gun hand (Figure 95), then proceed as described in the previous instruction.

Pistol-in-Pocket

A gunman who conceals his pistol as shown in Figure 96 is making it a little easier for you to disarm him. Once you actually commence your counterattack, it will be impossible for the gunman to redirect his weapon.

The first move is a jarring smash to the shoulder above the gun hand (Figure 97). The second move is a quick step toward the gunman combined with a chop across the nose or throat (Figure 98). Follow up with rips, blows, tears, and kicks to the assailant.

Two-Handed Pistol Grip

If a gunman confronts you with a double-handed pistol grip (as shown in Figure 99 or a variation

Figure 94.

Figure 95.

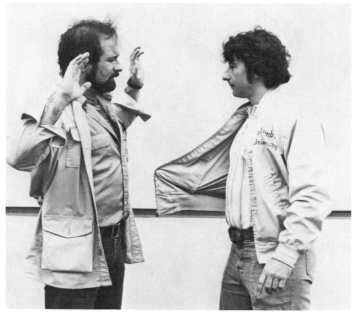

Figure 96.

Figure 97.

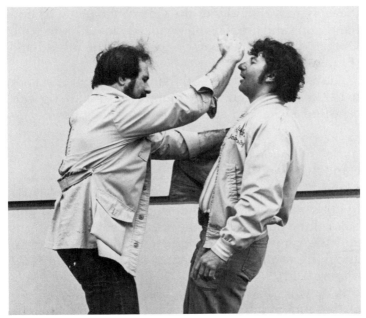

Figure 98.

Figure 99.

thereof), move rapidly to the side of the pistol as one hand grips and presses the weapon aside (Figure 100). Chop to the neck, throat, or nose with the other hand (Figure 101).

Grab the pistol with both hands and deliver a kick to the knee of the gunman (Figure 102). Follow up with repeated kicks and strikes when he goes down.

REAR HANDGUN DISARMING

Hands Up Position

Glance quickly over your shoulder (Figure 103) to determine which hand the gun is in, the size and build of the gunman, and the distance between yourself and the gunman. Pivot suddenly and sweep down, knocking aside the gun hand with a chopping blow (Figure 104).

If, as you turn, you find yourself practically on top of the gunman, proceed with an immediate knee to

Figure 100.

Figure 101.

Figure 102.

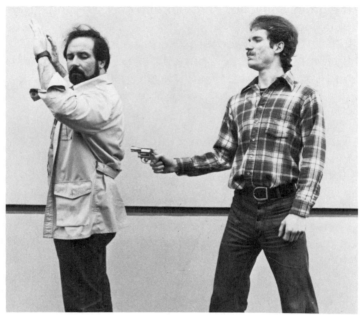

Figure 103.

Figure 104.

the groin, and follow through with chin jabs and an eye-gouging attack.

Basically, proceed with the same follow-up as in the first frontal technique, once the pistol is knocked aside and you have turned to face the gunman.

Hands Down Position

The hold-up position is shown in Figure 105. Pivot and knock aside the gun (Figure 106). If you pivot and block the gun hand with your left arm (assuming a right-handed gun threat), follow-up is with a fast right-hand chop across the nose or throat of the opponent. Grip the gun. Break the opponent's leg with a left stamp kick to the knee or shin and then follow through in the same manner as for the frontal threat with hands down.

If you pivot and block with the right arm (Figure 107), proceed instantly to follow through in the same manner as above, but with the opposite arm and leg.

Figure 105.

Figure 106.

Figure 107.

Pistol Aimed at the Face and Lapel Grab

When the gunman grabs your lapel and puts the pistol in your face (Figure 108), sweep the pistol outward, coverering the attacker's lapel grip with your right arm (Figure 109). Obtain a second grip on the gun hand with your left hand (Figure 110) and powerfully chop at the gunman's throat or nose, using the right hand. Then knee the groin (Figure 111).

SPECIAL SITUATIONS

Even when an experienced gunman holds the officer at gunpoint, keeping the pistol well back and staying out of arm's reach, there is a chance for survival. Obviously, a man who knows enough to hold a victim under proper control will also be very alert and cautious, so the chance of success is only 50 percent. However, if we know we are going to be shot anyway, we should welcome a 50 percent chance to live over virtual certainty that we will die.

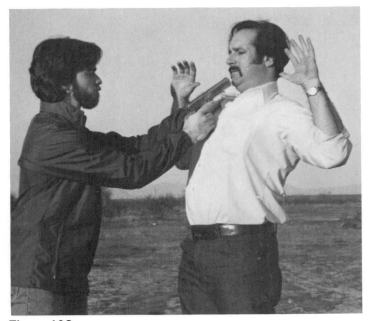

Figure 108.

Figure 109.

Figure 110.

Figure 111.

By suddenly diving directly to the side of the hand-gun pointing at you, straight for the attacker, you will at least close the gap between the gunman and yourself, and make body contact. By risking a crease from the gun's discharge, you give yourself the opportunity to cripple the gunman; under the circumstances, it is a reasonable trade-off.

A degree of luck, and a savage will to win, coupled with the great speed that only practice can make possible, just could turn the tables in your favor, even under this difficult threat. Remember: Once body contact is made the opponent must be destroyed. Hesitation here is simply suicide.

TAKING A PISTOL AWAY FROM A GUNMAN

I do *not* advocate this technique; however, the reported experiences of many reputable law-enforcement people has substantiated the possible need for this skill in police work, so it is included here. The object is to wrest the pistol away from the opponent and arrest him, without maiming or killing him. I feel obligated to warn the reader that to give breaks to opponents in hand-to-hand combat is to invite possible disaster.

Facing the gunman with the hands up (Figure 112), suddenly sweep your right hand down and grasp the attacker's gun wrist as you pivot inward (Figure 113). With your left hand grip the gun barrel (Figure 114) (this will not work with snubbies!) and jerk the barrel back, while snapping the gun wrist inward. This will break the opponent's trigger finger and cause considerable pain. Now, jerk the gun from his grip (Figure 115), and step back and hold the criminal at gunpoint, using the confiscated weapon.

Figure 112.

Figure 113.

Figure 114.

Figure 115.

11
The Shoulder-Weapon Attack

When you are facing a shotgun, rifle, submachine gun or sawed-off shoulder weapon of any type held by a man who intends to pull the trigger sooner or later, you are facing certain death unless you take effective action.

It is possible to be shot at point-blank range with a .38 revolver, say, and survive, but a load of 00 buckshot or .223, or a .308 cartridge at point-blank range can always be assumed to be fatal.

Effective disarming of a shoulder weapon does not depend on the type of shoulder weapon the gunman employs. Systems of disarming that vary according to the type of shoulder weapon are too complicated and unrealistic to use under actual combat conditions.

IMMEDIATE RESPONSE

Regardless of how the assailant "gets the drop" on the officer, it is essential that the officer not react hastily or foolishly. It is at the moment when the gunman confronts his victim that he has himself primed and ready for resistance, and a quick movement would only cause the gunman to jerk the trigger reflexively.

Upon confrontation, immediately accede to the

"hands up" or "don't move" command. If the gun is shoved or pressed up against your body, do *not* step back or touch the weapon. Be completely docile and accept the weapon's presence. Not only does this allay the gunman's anxieties, but it also is of enormous advantage in preparing a proper disarming move.

It is improbable that you will ever be ordered to assume the hands-behind-the-head or prisoner of war position. However, if you are, disarming may readily be commenced from it. If ordered to place your hands behind your head, do not interlace your fingers; rather, place your hands one over the other.

The advice given previously for handgun disarming is valid for shoulder-weapon disarming. When we compare disarming pistols or revolvers to disarming shoulder weapons, we find that there is one advantage the defender has against a shoulder weapon. Because a submachine gun, rifle, or shotgun is larger than a pistol, it is easier to ensure total control over the weapon.

Shoulder weapons are not as maneuverable as handguns, so once the defender jams the weapon aside and gains the upper hand, his success and survival are just about guaranteed, providing his basic hand-to-hand combat technique is sound.

The most dangerous and maneuverable shoulder weapons are the shortest. The riot-type shotguns having a barrel length of eighteen or twenty inches, the short machine pistols with real snubbie barrels, the carbines, and chopped-down weapons all pose the greatest problem for the defender. Longer rifles and shotguns are more unwieldly and present plenty of iron to hold onto. (A tip-off that the criminal may be an amateur is his use of clumsy, inappropriate combat weaponry.)

CRIMINAL USE OF SHOULDER WEAPONS

As a weapon of offensive combat, the shoulder weapon is vastly superior to the handgun. Even in instances where the shoulder weapon and the handgun fire the same cartridge (say, the .44 Magnum load), the shoulder weapon has an undeniable edge for offensive tactical engagement.

Criminals do not generally carry shoulder weapons about with them except sometimes to robberies. They are most often used when terrorist acts are committed, such as assassination attempts and assaults on vehicles or buildings.

It is common for a shoulder weapon to be used when a group of people are to be held under restraint or control. Because it is likely that there will be other innocent victims around when he is held at the point of a shoulder weapon, the officer must plan beforehand to be ready for this contingency. Obviously, it makes a big difference whether no one or an innocent person is hit when the officer knocks a criminal's firearm aside and the gun goes off. It would create a tactical advantage to time your attack so that, should the weapon go off, one of the other criminals is struck by the bullet.

When a shoulder weapon is used to intimidate by its mere presence, you have an advantage. For example, no kidnapper plans to kill his victim at the moment when the kidnapping is done. The kidnapper is therefore short-circuited in his effectiveness with any weapon he may have. The victim can and should use this fact to full advantage.

A kidnap victim, once taken to the hideout, stands little chance of survival. There is greater survival possibility by resisting violently at the time of the kidnap attempt. At worst, the victim's chances are 50-50 if he resists at the time of abduction. At best he stands an excellent chance of surviving and getting away (assuming he is trained in combat).

The various situations that may be encountered should be considered and thoroughly discussed in training. It is always very difficult to theorize when disarming should be undertaken and when the criminal's demands should be acceeded to. When money or property is clearly the only objective of the criminal, he should be given what he demands, with no opposition. When life is endangered, the criminal should be ruthlessly opposed.

One of the most valuable supplements to classes in disarming techniques is guest lectures: officers who have actually been held at gunpoint. It is an education to hear what these men have to say about their fears, their thoughts, their apprehensions, their physical stress sensations, etc. Naturally, any officer who has faced a gunman and disarmed him should be asked to speak to the recruits, and to be present as frequently as possible during actual classes when disarms are being taught.

12
Disarming the Shoulder-Weapon Attacker

The two basic principles of disarming technique remain the same: 1) Get out of the line of fire and/or knock aside the weapon, and 2) neutralize the gunman instantly. The disarming methods in this chapter are equally effective against a shotgun, rifle or submachine gun.

FRONTAL SHOULDER-WEAPON DISARMS

Weapon Aimed at Face

A gunman holds his weapon in front of your face, ordering "Hands up!" (Figure 116). Obey the command given by the gunman. Relax; muscular tension and psychological apprehension will decrease your chances of success and could easily telegraph your intentions to the gunman. If possible, the best strategy is to wait; when the gunman's mind is on what he is saying (possibly in answer to a question the defender has asked), *move!*

With lightning speed simultaneouly dodge to one side as you seize and turn aside the gunman's weapon (Figure 117). Kick hard into the assailant's crotch, knee, or ribs while retaining a strong grip on the weapon (Figure 118). Still holding onto the weapon, kick the

Figure 116.

Figure 117.

Figure 118.

attacker again, and moving in fast, smash a backfist or forearm blow across the temple area (Figure 119). Follow-up the initial counterattack by ripping at the gunman's eyes and/or throat while he is jerked and tripped. While holding onto the shoulder weapon, pull up as you stomp down with your heel into his head, kidney, groin or ribs. Only after the gunman has been incapacitated should the officer take away the weapon and arrest the gunman.

The above defense (and all of the defenses, in fact), should also be practiced with an "innocent" third party and even a fourth party present. This will train the officer to gauge his initial parry so that the weapon is not inadvertently whipped into a position where a bystander(s) might be shot.

Weapon Aimed at Midsection

This time the weapon is aimed at the solar plexus or the center of the officer's body. Assume that the

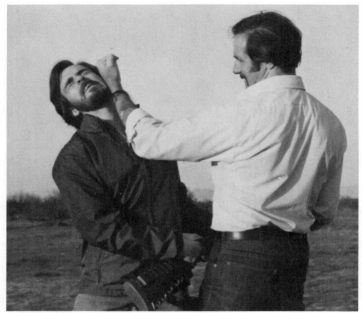

Figure 119.

officer will be facing a right-handed gunman.

The first move is a downward left-hand sweep block, coordinated with a hard kick into the gunman's groin with your left foot. As the kick lands, seize the weapon with your right hand and whip a vicious left-hand chop to the neck, throat, nose, or temple of the gunman.

A second kick with your left foot continues the attack, as your right hand retains control over the weapon. This second kick will be either into the gunman's groin or a stamp-type kick into the knee/shin area that concludes by crushing the instep.

Follow up with attacks until the gunman is harmless.

Variation Defense for Weapon Aimed at Midsection

This variation calls for you to commence with a right-hand sweep block (Figure 120). The block needs to be coordinated with a quick pivotal body movement to evade the muzzle of the weapon. Break the gunman's leg with a hard side kick, while retaining a tight con-

Figure 120.

Figure 121.

trolling grip on the weapon (Figure 121). The target for the kick is the knee and shin area. Quickly, move in close after the kick lands and snap a vicious left front-kick into the assailant's groin (Figure 122). Retain a hard grip with the left hand while the kick is delivered, and your right hand drops free.

Suddenly crack the opponent's left ear with a right-hand palm blow or chop his neck or temple with a hand-edge blow (Figure 123). Following the right-hand attack, rip at the gunman's face or eyes with the same hand. Jerk him to the ground with a trip while retaining a hold on the weapon. Finish by stomping the gunman's head, ribs, or groin, and finalize the arrest.

Weapon Several Feet Distant

This time there is some distance between the gunman and the officer (Figure 124). Execute an inward block with the foot sole, knocking the shoulder weapon to one side (Figure 125). Lunge forward as the kick

Figure 122.

Figure 123.

Figure 124.

Figure 125.

averts the gun barrel. Obtain any possible grip on the weapon and proceed to execute attacks (Figure 126). Let the position that results from the lunge determine what attacks to follow with.

The gunman has the advantage when the shoulder weapon is out of reach. However, once the officer moves in, it is almost impossible for the gunman to shift his weapon and body position in time to avoid the counterattack. A shoulder weapon is just too unwieldly. It goes without saying that any disarming attempt when the opponent is out of reach is risky. But it will succeed, if the gunman is caught off-guard.

REAR SHOULDER-WEAPON DISARMING

Weapon Pressed Against Back

A gunman presses the barrel against the officer's back (Figure 127). First, surrender totally. Raise your arms and relax. Offer an immediate verbal response indicating total submission.

Figure 126.

Figure 127.

As you give up to the gunman, glance over your shoulder. Look at the position, stance, size, and distance of the gunman. The time to move is not when you're confronted. Move when the gunman's wariness has relaxed, and, if at all possible, when his mental focus is clearly drawn elsewhere.

When your judgment tells you that the situation is right to move, your first action, with lightning speed, should be a swift rearward and sideways pivot and a snapping downward blow with the arm (Figure 128). As you turn, move *in,* toward the gunman, hooking the barrel of the weapon between your forearm and bicep muscle (Figure 129).

With your free hand, chop hard across the throat, temple, side of the neck, or nose of the opponent (Figure 130), and deliver a second chop in rapid succession, preferably to the same target struck by the first blow.

Figure 128.

Figure 129.

Figure 130.

Seize the shoulder weapon and, with both hands maintaining a controlling grip, deliver a side kick against the gunman's knee or shin area (Figure 131). This kick should continue down the gunman's shinbone and crush his instep.

Strike with the elbow against the gunman's face, while the opposite hand grips the weapon (Figure 132). Jerk the weapon from the gunman's hands as he falls and jab his face with the butt of the weapon. Kicks and stomps complete the disarm.

Variation Defense for Weapon Aimed at Back

In this case, the weapon may not be actually touching the officer's back.

Glance back! Pivot, suddenly sweeping one arm down and knocking the gun barrel aside. Capture the barrel of the weapon by seizing it with the opposite hand to the one that executed the block.

Kick either in a downward side-stamping fashion,

Figure 131.

Figure 132.

breaking the gunman's knee, or in a whipping front-kick manner, crushing his testicles with your instep.

Deliver a backfist smash or a bottomfist smash to the nose or temple, as the other hand retains a powerful grip on the weapon. Obtain a two-hand hold on the weapon and literally "kick the opponent free." Complete the disarm by stomping the opponent senseless.

Weapon Aimed at Head

A gunman aims his weapon at the officer's head from behind (Figure 133). The first move of the defensive sequence is a dodging pivot; at the same time, swing the arm high and over the weapon (Figure 134). As the arm sweep and pivot are executed, catch the weapon's barrel. A hard front-kick into the groin, ribs, or midsection must follow the arm sweep instantly (Figure 135). As the kick snaps back and is returned to the ground, kick with the other foot.

Grasp the weapon with both hands and, if the oppo-

Figure 133.

Figure 134.

Figure 135.

nent is still retaining a grip on his weapon, execute a leg-breaking side kick. Jerk the weapon free of the gunman as he falls, and smash his kidney with the gun's butt. Then apply stomps and kicks.

BAYONET DEFENSE

Although Combato's repertoire includes extensive defenses against an opponent who attacks with a shoulder weapon and bayonet (in a charging or thrusting fashion), this is really a military skill and is not applicable to police-training programs.

13
Basic Principles and Additional Applications

The key points made in this book concern physical and psychological preparedness.

Physically:
1. Block, avert, parry, dodge, knock aside, sidestep, avoid, or gain a controlling grip on the weapon-bearing arm or the weapon itself.
2. Neutralize the assailant instantly.

Psychologically:
1. Work through, analyze and conquer the innate Western cultural tendency to fear death.
2. Learn lucidity of perception via mental and physical relaxation and the maintenance of an empty, non-grasping, Ch'an state of mind.
3. Develop utter ruthlessness as your fighting attitude. Cultivate animalistic fury as the natural, immediate, and reflexive response to sudden life-threatening danger.
4. Fight ferociously and mercilessly, but without becoming emotionally involved in the outcome of the combat.

Pupils of disarming need to assimilate these main points because, to be effective with the skills of disarming, they must be able to modify and improvise.

The ability to modify comes only with a full understanding of what makes a specific defense or offense
work. No two situations will ever be the same in a fight.
It is unrealistic to expect otherwise. After mastering
the material in this book, the officer will be in a position to feel intuitively what general principles are
needed to effect a good technique. This takes time.

Physical and psychological aspects blend together
and are interdependent for success in actual application. For instance, the first physical principle of
Combato's disarming method (blocking, averting, etc.)
is dependent upon the following psychological factors
for success:

Conquest of the fear of death. When true peace of
mind is achieved in the face of death, there is no hesitation whatsoever in actually carrying out the block,
the parry, etc.

The Ch'an mental state. With this comes the lucidity and calmness of mind that permit's one's body to
move, machinelike, into perfect action.

Ruthlessness as a natural response. When this attitude predominates, there is no foolish "block" holding
the defender back. The thought of injuring or killing
the gunman becomes irrelevant.

Furious but emotionally detached action. This allows
the initial move of the disarming technique to be carried out without any anxiety. It permits the one doing
the disarming to attack all-out, without his mind being
clouded by fears or doubts.

Now, consider how the psychological factors augment the second principle of physical technique application, neutralizing the assailant:

Conquest of the fear of death. Clearly, a defender who
has overcome fear of death can concentrate totally
upon taking the offensive and neutralizing the attacker.
Death may well result from an overconcern with what
"might happen if. . ." and hesitation in launching the
counteroffensive. By overcoming the death fear one
releases one's ability to fight offensively and effectively.

The Ch'an mental state. With a nongrasping and calm mind, the officer can move quickly and improvise fluidly in the attacking sequences.

Ruthlessness as a natural response. With ruthless abandon (not *reckless*) the officer has no mental or emotional blocks to dealing out the full course of counterattacking punishment that the situation demands.

Furious but emotionally detached action. This psychological principle enables the defender full use of strength and skill under the stress of combat, and a clear understanding of the total situation, no matter how fast or furious the action is.

The secret of emotional detachment while being physically immersed in violent action is one of the most valuable for survival in combat. Realistic training to some extent aids its development, but the student's clear awareness of the need for this principle is one priceless aid in its acquisition.

In approaching the serious study of close combat and disarming, the student should be encouraged by the instructor always to be aware of the basic principles.

There can never be a guarantee of success in combat, and thorough mastery of the principles in this book will not alter this fact. However, there is certainly a greater likelihood of survival and victory in combat for the *trained* person than there is for the untrained one. The better the training the greater the chances for survival.

APPLYING THE BASIC PRINCIPLES

A limiting method of self-defense places serious restrictions on the practical adaptability of whatever specific techniques it espouses. Regrettably, this is one main fault of the popular classical martial art systems and methods, including judo, jujitsu, kempo, kung fu, karate and aikido. Combato, as a pure defense method, aims to avoid falling into this weakness, which is inherent in too many systems.

Combato is not a dogmatic system. It is closed only in one sense: It is unreceptive to sporting competition aims, methods, and procedures. Insofar as defense, personal protection, and survival are concerned, the system can add virtually any effective technique or strategy, so long as it meets the acid test of *working in combat.*

Combat is fluid, never static. Moves and strategies of the opposition in a fight are difficult to predict, and an effective method must take cognizance of this fact.

Though we may acquire definite and specific techniques, unless these techniques are adaptable to a variety of circumstances, they are not wholly reliable. If a technique is impossible to modify without destroying its effectiveness, then the technique, however impressive, is not a good one.

The student's introduction to improvisation should be formally taught only after considerable development of basic skills. Every student who trains with any degree of alertness will realize naturally that improvisation is possible, and sometimes more comfortable. However, in order to ensure a solid foundation in workable techniques, students should be told to experiment and modify only after they have genuine skills with which to work. This is advanced training.

Razor Defense

There are two ways in which the barber's straight razor may be used as a weapon: 1) It can be slashed, like a saber, the blade inflicting long gashes (generally not too deep); and 2) It can be used like brass knuckles, folded across the fist so the force of the punch drives the razor's blade deep (usually into the face).

The shock of being slashed with a razor can be worse than the actual physical damage done. Naturally, a razor can kill if it cuts deeply through the neck or the throat; however, more often than not, razor wounds are not fatal.

The best defense against a razor is alertness that

forewarns the officer of an attack. At the first hint of a criminal reaching for a weapon, the proper response is a forceful kick into the testicles.

Defense against a wild razor slash should take the form of a block or dodge of the criminal's weapon-bearing arm, followed by an instant counterattack, preferrably begun with a hard, leg-breaking kick. Repeated attacks must follow to ensure that the assailant's body and will are totally destroyed.

Chain Defense

Get so close that an attacker cannot swing the chain, or so far back that it doesn't matter if he does. Here again, Combato's principle obtains: First, avoid the weapon's immediate threat; second, neutralize the attacker.

Do not use one arm as bait when fighting against a chain-swinging attacker, as some methods advocate. A chain that wraps forcibly around your arm will break that arm—unless of course your arm is first wrapped in a jacket.

Close in with all possible speed after the chain-swinger launches his swing. Go for eyes, throat, etc., and do not relent.

Baseball Bat

A baseball bat is a brutally effective weapon and is commonly used by street gang members because it is not a weapon under the law, and may be carried quite openly with no chance of arrest.

The same principle as in defending against a chain applies to a bat. Get in or get back, then attack.

The swing radius of a bat is wide, but a trained man with normal reflexes can spin away or leap backward in time to avoid being hit. If the attacker is close to the officer, the officer should move in aggressively. An immediate and furious follow-up is in order.

Broken Bottle

When a potential attacker readies himself by breaking a bottle, take advantage of this time to break his leg. The bottle used as a bludgeoning weapon should be dealt with as a club; the broken bottle should be handled like a knife attack.

Hatchet

A hatchet blow cannot be effectively blocked once momentum is gained. Too much weight augments the swing; even if the arm's path were effectively blocked, the hatchet itself could swing free of the blocked arm and strike the victim.

If the attack is caught as the assailant raises his arm, then a hard, fast block will be successful. If the hatchet is in motion, do not attempt a block. Dodge to the side, fast, and then spring instantly into a counterattack.

SUMMING UP

The basic techniques and principles of Combato can be applied to any type of weapon attack situation. Further variation, even adapting the techniques to defend against multiple armed assailants, is simple. (With multiple armed attackers it is especially important not to choreograph set sequences of moves.) The defender merely faces a group of fellow trainees armed with mock weapons and allows them to move in. Then, reflexes dictate action. This is very advanced training.

Always remember that *simplicity* is the key to speedy, effective physical techniques.

14
Guidelines for Instructors

Expertise in performance of technique, alone, does not qualify a person to teach. This fact must be understood and fully appreciated by anyone charged with training others in hand-to-hand combat and disarming skills.

A good teacher of disarming should be able to perform whatever he teaches, but he should also be able to describe method and instruct others clearly.

What does make a good teacher of hand-to-hand combat, martial arts, or disarming skills? Just about the same things that make a good teacher of anything, actually. These are the qualifications that I would require of a Combato instructor, at black-belt level, before certifying him or her to teach:

1. Excellent ability to communicate verbally, both with individuals and groups, in a clear, well-modulated voice.
2. Ability to work with all kinds of people; a high tolerance for different cultures, belief systems, and ideas.
3. A genuine desire to help those whom he teaches, and a sense of satisfaction derived from making the effort.
4. Patience—*lots* of patience.

5. Complete absence of egotism or a sadistic need to show-off at the expense of pupils.
6. A firm, strong, but gentle nature.
7. A physically fit, agile and healthy body.
8. Knowledge of how to execute techniques with a high degree of expertise, and a commitment to retain and improve his own skill level.
9. Good working knowledge of human psychology—especially developmental and motivational psychology. Also, a good grasp of abnormal psychology and psychopathy.
10. Working knowledge of first aid and resuscitation methods.
11. Tact.
12. Sense of humor.

Any person who had a high degree of attainment in those twelve areas, and who had achieved the rank of first degree black belt in Combato (which would take a highly motivated student about four to five years) would certainly be seriously considered for certification as a teacher of Combato. This assumes, of course, that the individual *wants* to teach. I think one of the reasons for the disgracefully low quality of martial arts instruction generally available in this country is the requirement that black belts teach. Attainment of a black belt says nothing about a person's qualifications as a teacher.

A teacher, good or bad, has an enormous influence on his students. In the martial arts, which necessarily deal with combat skills, it is crucial that only benevolent and capable people teach—not only in police forces, but in society generally.

HOW TO CONDUCT A CLASS

The majority of people in an academy hand-to-hand class will be nervous at the outset of training. It behooves the instructor to respect this nervousness, help students acknowledge and face it, and point out calmly that it is a good thing, because it indicates that some real learning can take place.

As nervousness gives way to confidence the pupils will have learned two lessons: They will have acquired new skills, and they will have learned that apprehension can be dealt with rationally and creatively.

An instructor who belittles or intimidates the slower, more apprehensive students is not a true teacher. The responsibility of the instructor is to build confidence in his charges, not destroy it or undercut it. Too many really incompetent instructors (in both the armed and unarmed martial arts) use overbearing rudeness and plain bullying to mask their own inadequacies.

Classes should be as small as possible. The author prefers classes of between five and ten people, with twenty people being considered a very large class. A really good teacher can instruct more than twenty at a time, but to benefit the students most, such large classes should have at least one qualified assistant instructor for every ten people in excess of twenty. *It is extremely dangerous to allow people to practice the unrestricted combat skills described in this book with less than adequate supervision.*

The class should be held with the students seated comfortably in front of or around the instructor. Either an assistant instructor or a student should be used to demonstrate, and then analyze, every technique under study that day.

I suggest this procedure for demonstrating:

1. Call the class to attention.
2. Announce the subject of the lesson at hand. Before proceeding, ask the students if they understand the day's objective, and find out if anyone has any questions about what they will set out to accomplish that day. Encourage questions; be clear in replying.
3. Demonstrate the technique in slow motion.
4. Repeat a slow-motion demonstration. Call the

students' attention to all of the key points of the technique during this second demonstration. Verbally clarify why each movement is done the way it is done. Explain the effect of the action on the attacker.

5. Repeat the technique again, this time at about 50 percent speed and force, naturally taking care to keep all damaging blows short of contact.

6. Review with a final slow motion demonstration, again emphasizing the key points of the skill being taught.

7. Order the class to pair off and prepare to rehearse the technique. There must be ample space between students; if there is not, have some students sit and wait while the others drill.

8. Only when the instructor is satisfied that all of the students know what they are to do should anything faster than slow-motion practice be allowed. The instructor and the assistant(s) should move alertly and freely among the student pairs and try to catch and correct all errors immediately, as they occur. Calmly, clearly demonstrate on the spot how it should be done.

9. After physical drill, the students should be seated and have a quiet session of mental imagery training, during which they vividly review, in their mind's eye, the techniques that they have been drilling. Five minutes of this is plenty—and should be done with students' eyes closed. Following this imagery training, students should arise and drill again in the techniques.

10. A question-and-answer period should follow every class.

Contrary to the "macho" attitude generally (and erroneously) encouraged in many martial arts schools, I am in favor of coddling beginners. Some potentially fine students are alienated at the outset of many training programs simply because they are nervous or slow learners. Slow learning is not poor learning. Obviously, a student who is apprehensive and awkward after several weeks of training has serious problems, and it is questionable if such a person has what it takes to be a line police officer. But a student who commences training in a seemingly frazzled state should not be written off as hopeless until given a fair chance.

It is to a teacher's credit when a class graduates with slow learners able to do what only the fast learners could do at first.

ADVANCED STUDENTS

No police officer is ready to go out on the job without knowing what it is like to get cursed, belted around, and physically traumatized, and to remain undaunted and fight back in spite of it all.

This does not imply that deliberate maltreatment of officer-trainees is justified. It is not. However, a progression of tough, realistic training that builds the courage to fight a dangerous criminal and win is needed.

There are two activities that I believe are necessary in a complete hand-to-hand combat program for police recruits: basic boxing and pugil stick bouts.

Boxing is not fighting. However, punching and being punched (with head and teeth protection) is extremely valuable in building confidence and aggressiveness in recruits.

The combat instructor should know and be able to teach fundamental boxing; if he can't, professional instruction should be obtained. Five hours of boxing experience during an academy program is sufficient for each recruit.

Pugil stick bouts may be used in the same way and for the same basic purpose that they are used in Army Ranger training—to instill confidence and aggressiveness and the will to win. Twelve bouts per recruit during the academy course is plenty. The United States Army

Field Manual 21-150 (Combatives) should be obtained for full details on pugil technique.

By the way, all that has been said about hand-to-hand training, including the boxing and pugil bouts, applies to women officers as well if they are to be assigned street or patrol vehicle jobs or detective work. Special emphasis must be given to training women in how to cope psychologically with the inevitable verbal harrass-ment that will come from the people with whom she'll deal. Psychologists may be able to lecture effectively concerning this.

RELATIONS WITH STUDENTS

An effective instructor actively looks for things to praise about his students' progress. Errors should be carefully corrected, but never dwelled upon.

Cursing and ridicule are indicative of a serious defi-ciency in the teacher.

Disarming instructors should be living examples of physical and mental fitness. They should actively encourage students to become and remain totally fit by participating in lifetime fitness programs.

An instructor considering how best to approach a student concerning a particular problem should think, "If *I* were the student, and if *I* were having this same difficulty, how would *I* want to be approached by my teacher?" An honest answer to that question will sug-gest some good ways to approach the student.

ORGANIZING THE CLASS

Sufficient time must be set aside for training and practice. The usual routine followed by most police academies is grossly inadequate.

Twenty pupils taught by a capable teacher will learn quite adequately in three or four training classes a week of one and one-half to two and one-half hours' dura-tion. That is *not* too much time. A thorough class warm-up is necessary, plenty of demonstration and practice time is needed, and a break of ten to fifteen minutes midway in a class is desirable. Also, questions and answers are crucial in effective teaching. Students cannot afford to have their doubts and questions clarified by a street attack after they leave the academy! The time to ask and answer questions, and address particular learning problems, is during the academy program.

SAFETY

An instructor who injures a student during a demonstration or practice session will have a very negative effect not merely on the injured student, but on the entire class. There is never an excuse for carelessness in martial arts training.

The need for safety and respect toward one's fellow recruits in training must be stressed and actively demonstrated by the teacher. This is neither competitive judo nor tournament karate; it is a potentially lethal body of knowledge that is, by its very nature, designed to inflict grievous injury when applied. No less than when a recruit is taught to use a service sidearm, he must be indoctrinated in proper safety procedures.

Athletic supporters are highly recommended for male recruits, as are properly manufactured mats for the gym floor.

Lethal blows must *never* be practiced without pulling them short of contact, even when not delivered at full speed! Remember that even light attacks to the throat, eyes, testicles, knees, etc., can produce excruciating pain and, sometimes, permanent damage.

Students *must* get the experience of striking with their "personal weapons." They do not receive this in boxing or pugil bouts; they get it from pounding away at heavy striking bags, punching posts and other training aids. The attacks cannot be practiced against a live person, so this aspect of training is very important.

Finally, the instructor should remember that the goal is to prepare every recruit to face the most desperate conditions of close combat with society's proven enemies and emerge a winner—every time.